Women, Information Technology, and Scholarship

women, information technology, scholarship

Women, Information Technology, and Scholarship Colloquium
Center for Advanced Study
Urbana, Illinois

edited by
H. Jeanie Taylor,
Cheris Kramarae,
and Maureen Ebben

Publication of this work was supported in part by a grant from the George A. Miller Endowment.

For information write: Women, Information Technology and Scholarship Colloquium
Center for Advanced Study, 912 West Illinois Street
Urbana, Illinois 61801

Consultants: Dale Spender, Betsy Kruger, Brinlee Kramer

Designers: Kathleen Chmelewski, Nan Goggin

First edition
Printed in the U.S.

ISBN# 1-882875-00-1

LC 92-062491

PREFACE

This volume is an introduction to the Women, Information Technology, and Scholarship (WITS) working colloquium held at the Center for Advanced Study, University of Illinois at Urbana-Champaign. WITS grew from an idea conceived in April 1991 to an energetic collaboration of women that continues to grow and prosper.

As with much feminist publishing, this volume does not fit neatly into any traditional genre. We began this publication as an annual report for participants in the WITS colloquium and for the other UIUC faculty and administrators who want to know about the policy issues we are addressing. However, the many inquiries we received from researchers and administrators on other campuses in the U.S. and abroad made us realize that this publication should also be made available to all those concerned about the politics of information technologies processes.

In our literature searches, we had difficulty finding publications that deal directly with the ways gender, race, and class hierarchies are made part of the circuitry in the new information technologies as they are used on campuses. Individually, we knew some of the problems, but we did not see our knowledge reflected in campus policies or in communication research. For example, we see many academic publications dealing with computers, knowledge, and intelligence, but few dealing with sexual harassment or with sexual division of labor in designing, using, and evaluating computer systems. We know that often our knowledge is not recognized as such in many committees dealing with plans for library reorganization. We know that many campus discussions about new information technologies are actually discussions about the reconstitution of race, sex, and class hierarchies in the new systems. In sum, the new developments are having major, often unforeseen, consequences for the politics of gender, race, and class in universities.

We realize that our discussions here are as far from comprehensive as are most other academic discussions of the new communication technologies. (While race, gender, and class are, of course, integrated hierarchies, we have focused primarily on gender in our WITS meetings and workshops. We have not yet dealt with many vital issues, including employment. Our beginning discussions help show the gaps and lapses in our work.) However, the following essays, bibliographies, and digests introduce issues that we believe are central to decision-making at all universities in the U.S.

CONTENTS

	3	Preface
	7	Women, Information Technology, and Scholarship (WITS): An Introduction
	9	WITS Colloquium Schedule 1991-1992
Articles	15	Women and Information Technologies: Creating a Cyberspace of Our Own **Maureen Ebben and Cheris Kramarae**
	28	Electronic Scholarship: Perform or Perish? **Dale Spender**
	44	Networked Serials, Scholarly Publishing, and Electronic Resource Sharing in Academic Libraries: A Dilemma of Ownership **Ann L. Okerson**
	52	Women and Men on Electronic Networks: A Conversation or a Monologue? **Cheris Kramarae and H. Jeanie Taylor**
Colloquium Digests	62	WITS Colloquium Digests
	63	Changes in Academic Concepts of Privacy, Originality, and Ownership of Ideas **Dale Spender**
	65	Publishing in an Electronic Environment **Phyllis Hall**
	67	Imagining the Ideal Information Technology **Marie T. Banich and Betsy Wilson**
	68	Talking on InterChange **Gail Hawisher**
	70	Linking Women: Computer Networks as a Feminist Resource **Judy Smith**
	72	Agency in the Age of Information **H. Patricia Hynes**
Addendum	75	WITS and the Joint Academic Network (JANET) **Jo Kibbee**
	76	Designing a Visual Identity: Empathic Response to Content **Kathleen Chmelewski and Nan Goggin**
Bibliography	78	Women and Information Technology: An Annotated Bibliography **Maureen Ebben and Maria Mastronardi**
Participants	122	WITS Participants 1991-1992
Contributors	125	List of Contributors

The Women, Information Technology, and Scholarship (WITS) colloquium, sponsored by the Center for Advanced Study, is an interdisciplinary group of faculty and academic professionals on the University of Illinois Urbana-Champaign campus, working to help insure that new communications technologies will be structured and used in ways beneficial and equitable for all.

The widespread interest in technological innovation on this campus and the support of a number of administrators provide us with an opportunity to develop analyses, programs, and policies that could be used on many other campuses as well.

Some of our overarching interests:

- *Responsibility toward future generations of university students and faculty*
- *Freedom of information for all citizens of all nations*
- *Easing rather than exacerbating the difficulties women and "minorities" face on campuses*
- *Availability of resources especially designed to benefit those who have found universities a largely hostile environment*
- *Respect for diversity in policy-making that involves information technologies*

Awareness of local, national, and global economic, social, and political inequities and of the ways the current and planned uses of information technologies will replicate or adjust those inequities.

We are aware that while these are our own major interests, they are not yet the goals of many of the policymakers of the larger society. In some cases lack of interest may be due to inertia or an unwillingness to reconsider the mission and practices of universities. In some cases it may be due to lack of respect for or knowledge of women's values, concerns, skills, perspectives, and experiences.

In our WITS sessions we discuss our concerns in order to share short- and long-term suggestions. Our discussions are based on presentations of guest lecturers; experiences of UIUC faculty, students, and academic professionals; workshops dealing with specific technological processes; and essays on "infotech" controversies. Some related activities have been open to the public, but the colloquium has been designed as an ongoing forum for a dedicated group of participants.

Some of the topics of the colloquium include changing concepts of privacy;

property rights in information; functions of university libraries; category systems for new databases; massive changes in the publishing world; possible de-skilling of professionals in "women's professions"; ethics of computer use; computers in classrooms; universities as publishers; harassment on electronic mail (e-mail) and networks; impact statements for evaluation of technology changes.

We would appreciate hearing from others working on related issues, and welcome all comments and suggestions that would add to this work.

1991-1992

Below is the program we followed during our first year.

25 September 1991 — *Topic:* How Can a Woman Hold a Library in Her Hand, and Why Would She Want To? (Introduction to WITS)
Speakers: Cheris Kramarae, 1991-1992 Center for Advanced Study Resident Associate and WITS coordinator, Professor of Speech Communication and Sociology, UIUC; Maureen Ebben, 1991-1992 Center for Advanced Study Graduate Research Assistant, Doctoral Candidate in Speech Communication, UIUC.

2 October — *Topic:* Campus Computing and Networking at the University of Illinois
Speaker: Leigh Estabrook, Chair, UIUC Committee on Computing and Networking; Dean, Graduate School of Library and Information Science.

16 October — *Topic:* Changes in Academic Concepts of Privacy, Originality, and Ownership of Ideas
Speaker: Dale Spender, scholar-at-large, Australia, is a cofounder of WITS and a graduate of universities in Australia and England. She is a feminist whose major research interest (in more than 20 books) has been to document the absence of a fair hearing for women and to assess the implications of this in relation to language, literature, history, technology, and the politics of knowledge in general. She was the founding editor of Women's Studies International Forum and Pandora Press in England, and has taught at universities in many countries.

30 October — *Topic:* New Technologies and the Classroom
Speakers: Nora Sabelli, Senior Research Scientist, National Center for Supercomputing Applications; Bob Jones, Director of the Hypermedia Lab and Professor of Sociology, UIUC.

13 November — *Topic:* Electronic Publishing for Academics: Threats and Opportunities
Speaker: Phyllis Hall, Staff Director of Publishing Services, Institute of

Electrical and Electronic Engineers, and former Senior Vice President of Pergamon Press; Carole Appel, Senior Editor, University of Illinois Press.

4 December — *Topic:* Electronic Access to Women's Studies Research
Speakers: Judith Hudson, Librarian, The University at Albany, State University of New York, and editor (with Steven Atkinson) of *Women Online: Research in Women's Studies Using Online Databases* (Binghamton, N.Y.: Haworth Press, 1990); Beth Stafford-Vaughan, Librarian, Women's Studies/Women in International Development, UIUC.

22 January 1992 — *Topic:* Champagne and Microchips: Imagining the Ideal Information Technology
A collaborative workshop was held to explore various aspects of the ideal information technology, using small group techniques.
Speakers: Betsy Wilson, UIUC Undergraduate Librarian, and Marie Banich, Associate Professor, Department of Psychology, Beckman Institute, UIUC.

5 February — *Topic:* Talking on INTERCHANGE
WITS met to experiment with INTERCHANGE, a synchronous network. Synchronous networks are now being used in writing classes to facilitate discussion and give students practice in writing. For our group, INTERCHANGE will allow us to talk all at once on any subject we wish. We came up with a list of ideas for creating a Center for Women, Technology, and Scholarship and then used INTERCHANGE to brainstorm about what such a center might do, discussing such issues as structure, goals, and funding sources.
Speaker: Gail Hawisher, Director, University of Illinois, Center for Writing Studies, and WITS member. Gail is coeditor of the journal *Computers and Composition: A Journal for Teachers of Writing* and of the book *Evolving Perspectives on Computers and Composition Studies: Questions for the 1990s.*

12 February — *Topic:* Women and the Networked Organization
In mixed-sex groups, women are often at a disadvantage. They talk less; their ideas are not fully credited; they influence the group less. Some characteristics of network communication obscure cues to the participants' gender, and in those situations women are not as disadvantaged. Lee Sproull described how computer discussion groups can function as electronic support groups.
Speaker: Lee Sproull, Professor of Management at Boston University's School of Management and coauthor of *Connections: New Ways of Working in the Networked Organization* (MIT Press, 1991).

19 February — *Topic:* Sex and the Nets: Issues of Censorship
E-mail and computer bulletin boards can be wonderful aids for women. However, they can be as genderized as other discussion forms. Women are reporting sexual harassment on many new networks (where ratios of men to women are often 20 to 1). Some network monitors censor sexist or obnoxious

comments. However, the values of the censor are often challenged. Also discussed was the case of the psychiatrist in his 50s who presented himself as a neuropsychologist in her 20s with serious disabilities, and formed intense on-line friendships and romances with dozens of unsuspecting women. *Speakers:* Cheris Kramarae and Maureen Ebben.

26 February *Topic:* Digital Photographs: Seeing is Believing?
WITS members Bea Nettles and Kathleen Chmelewski shared art and design work they have done utilizing computer programs.
Speakers: Bea Nettles has been Chair of the Photography Program at UIUC since 1984 and is a University Scholar. Kathleen Chmelewski has a joint appointment in Photography and Graphic Design and has worked extensively in both disciplines. Both are in the Department of Art and Design, UIUC.

4 March *Topic:* Academic Publications: Who Owns What in the Electronic Form?
For printed information, copyright is assigned to publishers, and libraries buy materials they can share within the definitions of "fair use." In the world of electronic information, publishers sell no artifact and libraries own nothing. Using a landlord-tenant analogy, Ann Okerson suggested that copyright makes us tenants of our own writing and offered ways this scenario might be altered.
Speaker: Ann Okerson, Director, Office of Scientific and Academic Publishing, Association of Research Libraries, Washington, D.C. She is actively involved with the evolution of academic publishing in the electronic age.

18 March *Topic:* Linking Women: Computer Networks as a Feminist Resource
The use of computer networks as tools for social change was discussed. Topics included experience linking women's organizations in Montana; Big Sky Telegraph; women as reluctant network users; ways to make networks more woman-friendly; and specific social change applications on the national network "Handsnet."
Speaker: Judy Smith, Project Director for WORD (Women's Opportunity Resource Development) in Missoula, Montana. WORD is involved in working on economic development and welfare reform and is part of Handsnet, a group of ten similar projects linked through electronic networks to facilitate collaboration. Judy has been involved in a number of educational projects on campuses and in communities that focus on feminist assessment of technology.

25 March *Topic:* Scientific Visualization
Scientific visualization is a process that changes information from a numerical or conceptual space into visual forms. These images have become part of scientific discourse, allowing researchers to "see" things they could not otherwise interpret easily from the data. Because methods of visual representation have so much impact on how data are interpreted, these methods become as important as the data themselves.

Speaker: Colleen Bushell, Visualization Group, National Center for Supercomputing Applications, UIUC.

8 April *Topic:* Agency in the Age of Information
Because of the combination of remote-sensing technology and global information-gathering networks, we are witnessing an almost infinite assemblage of images and data of the global environment. Most people herald the tidal wave of environmental information as education and consciousness-raising. A handful of critics call the explosion of urgency-laden information hyperbolic; others, apocalyptic. Few note that most environmentalists omit agency ("a minimum of 140 plant and animal species are condemned to extinction each day") or conflate agency with intermediate cause ("the underlying problem is growth in human population"). H. Patricia Hynes discussed some of the rigors feminists face in naming who does what to the environment.
Speaker: H. Patricia Hynes, Director of the Institute of Women and Technology and a faculty member of the Department of Urban Studies and Planning at the Massachusetts Institute of Technology. Her research focuses on women, technology, and the environment. She is currently working on a critique of the media and its presentation of science. Her books include *The Recurring Silent Spring*, a book about Rachel Carson and her work.

15 April *Topic:* Realizing the Ideal Information Technology
At this meeting we considered how material presented and discussed can be put to further use and explored some questions raised but not discussed in previous meetings.
Speakers: WITS members Ramona Curry, Assistant Professor of English, Susan Lamb, Associate Professor of Physics and Astronomy, and Marie Banich, Associate Professor of Psychology.

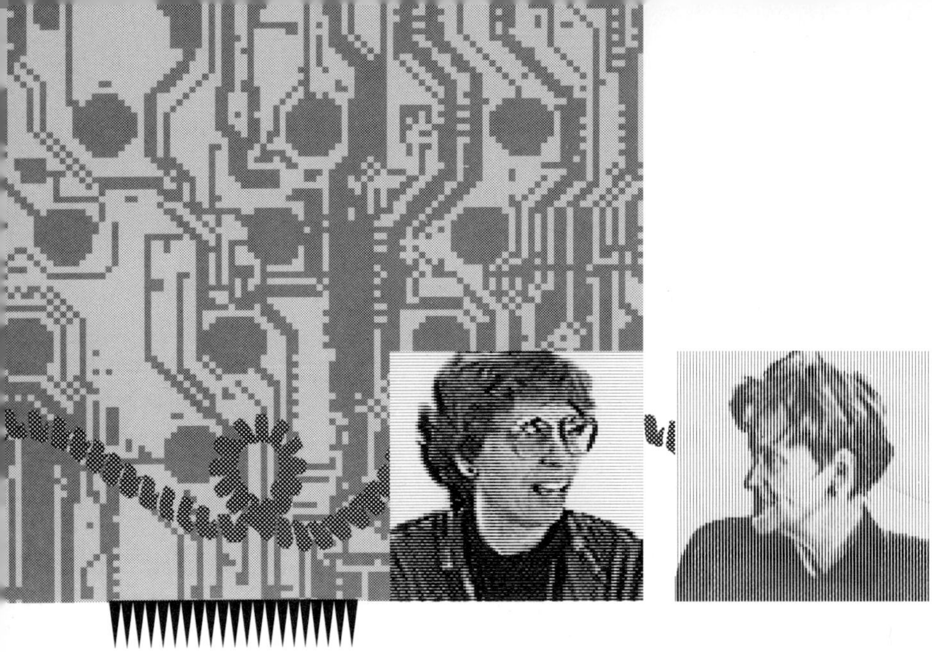

Women and Information Technologies: Creating a Cyberspace of Our Own

Maureen Ebben
Cheris Kramarae

Introduction

Given the historical relationship of women to male power and technology, the issues related specifically to women's entry into the information revolution need to be identified and evaluated. In this essay we focus on some of the key problematic issues faced by women as we try to establish our rightful place within the complex nexus of new information technologies. We've learned that once policy paths have been taken with new technologies, visible controversy and serious debates over social goals become very difficult, with critical voices being heard as irrational and irritating.

Although knowledge of information technology systems is now required for much academic work, examination of computer use reveals a great disparity between women and men. In part this is because there are not as many women in science fields, which make heavy use of the new technologies. In part the gap exists because girls and women do not receive as much training in and experience with computers in primary and secondary education, and this pattern continues in higher education.[1] There are race and class inequities as well in the use of computers.[2] On most campuses the science and technology information and policy-making groups are composed primarily of men. Although women are not usually deliberately excluded, many have been reluctant to raise concerns when they realize that few others in the group have had similar experiences with sex stratification, technology, and campus organizational structure and change.

Our challenge to the university is that women's voices not only be allowed, but be encouraged and listened to, during this time of rapid technological change. If the faculty and administration are really concerned about their stated goals of providing meaningful education to students from a variety of backgrounds, the material in this publication will be of interest. Understanding the issues presented here requires an interest in holistic approaches to the sociology of "scholarship" and the willingness to ask not how universities can help women overcome "deficiencies" in their education, but rather how universities are biased against women.

Although many have extolled the democratizing and emancipatory virtues of various forms of information technologies, we do not necessarily share this

1) In 1990, only 13% of U.S. computer science doctorates were awarded to women. The same year, less than 8% of all computer science professors in the U.S. were female (Ellen Spertus, 1992). For discussions of the reasons girls are dropping out of science and math in their early years even though they do well in it, and for descriptions of the very chilly climate for women in computer science, see Karen Frenkel, 1990; Nancy Leveson, 1989; and Amy Pearl et al., 1990.

2) Women are overrepresented on the global production lines of the computer industry, but are severely underrepresented in the top managerial positions (Ellen Spertus, 1991).

unabashed enthusiasm. Cognizant as we are of women's subordinate place vis-à-vis male technologies, our feeling can best be described as cautious optimism. That is, we acknowledge the powerful potential of new information technologies, but we are also painfully aware that many of these potentials have yet to be fully realized for women. This essay seeks to address this gap by identifying some of the important issues for women as we enter this new era. As members of a research and educational community, we believe that institutions of higher learning have a special responsibility to ensure equity of instructional quality for all. Our discussion focuses on four key areas: 1) problems of access and the difficulties encountered by women working in the various electronic forums; 2) shortcomings of mainstream information technology training methods; 3) paradoxes of the promises versus the actuality of information technology use in education; and 4) the changing face of electronic publishing.

Access and Electronic Forums

The difficulties of access to new information technologies for women occur at two levels. First, there is the problem of access in terms of sheer hardware and software. That is, can a woman at any given campus access the networked society of the future? Does she have the requisite software to support her communications? Does she have access to the knowledge and skills to use it? Many of the large universities in the United States have spent tens of millions of dollars to lay cables to link dormitories, offices, and classrooms to the national networks, but this is not the case at the smaller colleges where a disproportionate number of women carry on their research and teaching.

In addition to requiring access to the necessary hardware and software, women need access to meaningful resources about women. Access is meaningless if a woman in the English department can only connect with the engineering bulletin boards or the men's movement newsgroups. She needs to be linked to timely and relevant databases, bulletin boards, on-line library searches, and newsgroups. For example, compared to the hundreds of on-line discussion groups presently in existence, only a handful of these electronic forums are germane to the feminist scholar.[3]

To make matters worse, there is no guarantee that relevant and useful resources about women will appear unless women work, under often difficult situations, to create them. As the primary medium of information shifts from the printed page to the electronically produced screen, women's knowledge, which is presently encoded in books, may be endangered. As Dale Spender (1991) puts it, "[w]omen's knowledge is more at risk now than at any other period in our history." If the current trend continues and books are ultimately left behind as an old-fashioned, out-of-date form, it is crucial that the shift from the printed page to the electronically produced screen be made for women and feminist works. Of course, this is no easy endeavor, as currently there are few women in positions of leadership making the decisions about what electronic forums will be constructed and what they will contain.

3) The following electronically mediated organizations for women may be of interest. (These are in no particular order.)
soc.women–Moderated newsgroup for discussion of issues of concern to women.
soc.feminism–Moderated newsgroup for discussion of issues of concern to women.
Femecon-L–List for feminist economists.
gaynet–Moderated list for discussion of issues of concern to lesbians and gay men.
sappho–Moderated list for discussion of issues of concern to lesbians.
Gender–Moderated list for discussion of issues pertaining to the study of communication and gender.
WMST-L (Women's Studies List)–Moderated list for academic discussion of research and teaching in Women's Studies.
Systers–Network for female computer scientists. Provides forum for electronic mentoring. By invitation only.
GRANITE (Gender Relations and New Technology) –International network of scholars and policy makers.
Herstory–Women's history discussion group. This list is still in the planning stages.
Femail–Moderated newsgroup for discussion of issues of concern to women.
WON (Women's Online Network)–Distributes information, aids in the coordination of useful political action and provides a forum for developing strategies to improve the position of women in society.

Nonetheless, our task is clear: We need to create, electronically, a cyberspace of our own that fosters women's communication and scholarship in this time of rapid technological transition.

The fact that most computer networks are currently dominated by men raises further questions about women's access to new information technologies.[4] A recent study of a "friendly composition and rhetoric discussion group in which feminism enjoyed considerable influence" found that women contributed only 30% of the messages, and the women's messages were shorter and were not responded to as often as the men's (Susan Herring, Deborah Johnson, and Tamra DiBenedetto, 1992).[5] During a two-day period in which the women did post more messages than the men, the men responded angrily and some threatened to quit the group.[6] This research supports Dale Spender's (1989) thesis that when women speak more than 30% of the time (whether verbally or electronically) they are perceived as dominating. If this asymmetrical gender representation dictates topic choices and topic development in electronic discussion groups, how can women achieve full access? If some participants' interests are silenced, what does this say about the quality of the electronic "community?"[7] If the same positions of power are transferred intact to a new medium, what do we make of the arguments put forward for the democratizing effects of electronic communication?[8]

Although such evidence of women's unequal levels of participation on electronic discussions may appear disheartening, positive models of women's use of information technologies do exist. Just as women have appropriated telephone technology, which was developed strictly for commercial purposes, and used it as a means of building and sustaining human relationships (Lana Rakow, 1988, 1992), more recently women are moving into the realm of electronic communication technologies and using them for their own purposes. The Electronic Salon, hosted in April 1992 by Lewis and Clark College in conjunction with their Gender Symposium, is one such example. The Electronic Salon afforded a unique opportunity for academic women across the United States and the world to be electronically linked. Once connected to the Salon by means of electronic mail, the more than 200 participants could download the invited research essays on gender and technoscience and discuss the papers. (Deborah Heath, Sociology and Anthropology, Lewis and Clark College [heath@lclark.edu] planned this cyberspace for a computer-mediated discussion of invited papers.) The Electronic Salon provided a rare forum for the sharing of ideas and interests about women and information technologies as the usual constraints of time, money, and distance that frequently prevent women from attending an academic conference were significantly diminished. Moreover, because this electronic "gathering" was organized primarily by women, focused on women's issues, and had women as its main participants, it was potentially empowering. (However, there was a disparity between men's and women's participation rates. As the total number of messages from men increased during the week of the symposium, the participation of women decreased. Women appeared to be shut out of the discus-

4) Lee Sproull's (1992) study quantifies the male domination of computer networks at 95%. Our experience as readers of two network newsgroup forums specifically geared to women (soc.women and soc.feminism) corroborates these findings. For example, we have collected some amazing discussions in which men claim inordinate time and space and criticize the comments women do make. Susan Herring et al. (1992) report that female linguists on the LINGUIST electronic discussion list contributed significantly less than do male linguists–20% and 80% respectively–with women most noticeably silent in discussions of an abstract nature.

5) Not only did the women contribute significantly less than the men, but the length of women's messages were shorter than the men's. In addition, Herring, Johnson, and DiBenedetto found that the men got more responses to their messages than did the women. The most frequent direction of response was from men to men (33.4%), followed by women to men (21.3%), men to women (15.8%), and finally women to women (11.2%). Both men and women responded more to men, giving an indication of the more powerful status of men in the group overall (Susan Herring, Deborah Johnson, and Tamra DiBenedetto, 1992).

6) During the two-day period in which women posted more messages than the men, the women were responding to a man's suggestion about teaching a course on "men's literature." The women argued that the course could perpetrate male hegemony by coopting resources that could be used for women's literature courses. The men argued that they were denied an opportunity to discuss their gender identity (Susan Herring, Deborah Johnson, and Tamra DiBenedetto, 1992).

sions, which, as time went on, were increasingly dominated by the men.)

This instance of women's attempt to exploit the promise of computer-mediated exchange to foster women's communication and feminist scholarship points to the difficulty of the task we face. The old patterns of male control in conversation are well entrenched. Perhaps a social revolution in which women's conversational power is reasserted is needed more than an information revolution in which male control is perpetuated through different means. It may take more than a new medium to provide for equality in the messages. Nonetheless, this example of women's use of new information technologies points to the sort of action we believe needs to be taken to move women to greater participation in electronic forums. We need to think seriously about considering computer networks an additional feminist resource.

Failure of Training Programs

Ironically, the shortcomings of mainstream information technology training methods for women are many, despite the fact that the research on learning is well-developed and well-documented. We contend that the problem is not so much that we do not know how to teach people–especially women– effectively as much as that what is known by learning specialists rarely gets transferred and taken up by information technology trainers. The result is that most training is ad hoc and unsystematic. The "training" offered at computer sites at UIUC, for example, consists primarily of directions posted on computer room walls, photocopied sections of published manuals left in strategic places, or an hour's worth of group instruction in which participants are led though a manual's directives. Instruction is seldom customized and there is little opportunity for follow-up on questions and problems that arise during actual use. At this university, such scanty and unsystematic training frustrates women faculty, staff, and students, who frequently voice their complaints.

How is this lack of training a more severe problem for women than for men, who surely receive the same skimpy and unreliable instruction? To answer this question, we need to turn to a discussion of the culture that has arisen around information technologies. Sherry Turkle's (1984, 1988) work on the culture of computing provides the key insights. She writes that those engaged in the activity of computing are working within a culture that valorizes the intrepid adventurer. This culture has set the tone for many of the related cultures and practices surrounding the new information technologies to such an extent that if a person asks to be systematically taught new skills she may be regarded with disdain. Like the culture of computing, the culture of new information technologies shares an image of machismo (Sally Hacker, 1989, 1990). Why is this a problem for women? The difficulty for women is explained in good part when we realize that, on the whole, women and men tend toward quite different learning styles.

According to the research on learning, many women prefer to learn through an orderly routine in which they understand the reason for each step taken, whereas many boys and men have been encouraged to learn through

7) Cheris Kramarae and H. Jeanie Taylor, in an essay in this volume, discuss the problems of harassment encountered by women participating in electronic networks.

8) A representative example of the popular argument for the democratizing effects of electronic communication can be seen in the following quote from Sara Kiesler, Jane Siegel, and Timothy McGuire's (1991) report on the social and psychological aspects of computer-mediated communication. The authors write: "Once people have electronic access, their status, power, and prestige are communicated neither contextually (the way secretaries and meeting rooms and clothes communicate) nor dynamically (the way gaze, touch, and facial and paralinguistic behavior communicate). Thus, charismatic and high-status people may have less influence, and group members may participate more equally in computer communication" (p334). Our experiences and observations with computer-mediated communication render this statement highly problematic.

experimentation and trial and error (Sherry Turkle and Seymour Papert, 1990). Women are not so much interested in taking risks as they are in taking a systematic approach to learning. Men, on the other hand, prefer to tinker around in the new environment. The point here is not that one style is better than another, but rather that one style has been given preference over the other. Because training methods employed for various information technologies tend to be characterized by an unroutinized, unsystematic, and ad hoc approach, we can see how the learning programs have followed male-centered learning styles. What makes matters worse is that women, more than men, have learned to be hesitant and cautious about using new machinery. This, coupled with male-style learning practices, puts women at a disadvantage.

What is to be done? Our central concern is to put the training of information technologies into women's learning styles. Drawing on the exemplary training work done by Judy Smith (1992), project director for WORD (Women's Opportunity Resource Development in Missoula, Montana), our recommendation is twofold: first, skills need to be linked to rewards, and second, instruction needs to be systematic.

Skills should be more closely associated with rewards because significant rewards make the task worth accomplishing. To make this possible, skills need to be broken down into smaller units that can be learned and rewarded. Smith argues that "reluctant users," such as women and "minorities," are best taught the skills of using information technologies by provision of reinforcing rewards that are meaningful to them. For example, if a woman knows that the result of learning how to operate a computer network means that she will have another, quicker means of communication with specific colleagues at other universities, she will be more highly motivated to learn. Moreover, seeing the immediate benefit of her efforts will help her to continue using the technology.

Instruction needs to be systematic, with follow-up instruction provided to keep women's skills advancing. These simple recommendations help to translate what is known about effective instruction into the context of information technology training. If these suggestions were implemented, it is likely that women would be more interested and involved in gaining expertise with information technologies.

Classrooms – What is New About the New Technologies?

The new technologies are, of course, already changing university classroom-related activities and understandings about appropriate behavior. For example, use of computers makes it easier for teachers to update bibliographies and for students to compose and revise written assignments. Use of video cameras in Harvard classes revealed to teachers that male students were speaking up to two and a half times longer than female classmates in the most common classroom settings (i.e., male teacher and a majority of male students) (*Harvard Magazine,* March/April 1986).

Although these are valuable uses of information technologies, the benefits of these technologies are often overstated. An underlying assumption of many educators is that computers and multimedia possibilities of the new technologies are the most important part of the future of education. However, we do not simply argue that computers are magical, or sinister, but that the new information technologies hold a potential that is not fully realized for women. To better illuminate our claim, we discuss three of the prevalent assumptions about "education" and the use of computers in the classroom.

Argumentative Dueling

The first assumption is rooted in the notion that education is accomplished either through an adversarial method of teaching or by individual investigation. The "higher" the level of education, the more the teaching/learning model is based on a model of argumentative dueling, of marshaling arguments and applying them in force. In interviews, we find that white male students, in particular, talk about education in metaphors pertaining to war, such as the pleasure of "battling over ideas" and being able to "punch and jab" at the teacher's comments (Cheris Kramarae and Paula Treichler, 1990). White female students are more likely to talk about what they consider the lack of collaborative work, while many Hispanic and Native American students, female and male, feel that openly disagreeing with a teacher is a sign of disrespect. For these social groups, belonging and cooperation, rather than competition and individual achievement, are highly valued (Sara E. Meléndez and Janice Petrovich, 1989).

As mentioned above, individual learning is privileged in this first assumption, and we can see how this notion gets played out in the ways computers are implemented in the classroom. Whether through a lecture or a debate, the teacher regulates classroom talk. Usually, only one person speaks at a time, with the teacher responding between student comments. Extending this insistence on privileging the individual, advocates of computer use emphasize the computer's capacity for fostering individual instruction. Nolan Estes and Victoria Williams (1988) write:

> ... perhaps the most important... for educators is the ability of the computer to improve the individual instructional process. Students are able to interact one-on-one with a piece of equipment, and unlike other technologies, students can perceive valuable learning experiences pegged to their achievement and interest levels.... A friendly computer can do this all day long, with greater patience and without bias. (p246)

Although computers may have many worthwhile functions, friendliness isn't one of them. Even if they are well programmed they know little about users. (As Suzanne Damarin at Ohio State University points out [personal communication], users used to be called students– people who studied.) While students talk about the need for more attention from teachers and more cooperation among students, the computer experts' discourse is characterized by talk about the benefits of individual computerized instruction. Seldom have students actually requested computerized individual instruction. Rather, they have stressed the need for increased contact and communication but useful for memorization rote learning 18A

between teachers and students. Ironically, the shift in education toward computerized individual instruction serves to diminish, and perhaps ultimately eliminate, student-teacher interaction.

The presence of computers in the classroom results in other consequences unforeseen by computer advocates. Several teachers have reported on what happens when students were placed two to a computer, as happens when "not enough" computers are available. Students help each other in ways that are very different from the hierarchical, competitive activities of much of the rest of the school day. This was not by teachers' or computer experts' design but by students' design, and under conditions which students had little control. More thoughtful consideration needs to be given to the spatial arrangements and related dynamics of computer use in the classroom.

Knowledge Claims

The second assumption about education is rooted in the notion that knowledge is an accumulation of matter built up at universities that flows out to quench the intellectual thirst of all others. University facts, truths, wisdom– the highest knowledge – supposedly dribbles down, in simplified form to pupils in secondary and elementary schools and to people in "Third World" countries. Many educators talk about Knowledge as if it is clear, certain Fact, the sum total of what is Known. Rarely, however, is there mention about what is Known by whom: only that students using computers will be able to get more Knowledge, more swiftly, because Knowledge can be stored in computers to be retrieved at any time by anyone. The focus is on the quantity, not the quality, of Knowledge. For example, Michael L. Dertouzos (1991) writes in *Scientific American* about those possibilities for global influence:

> We [people in business, government, the professions and academic life] might even begin to collect the knowledge resources of our nation in a new kind of widely accessible electronic "Library of Congress." This leverage of increased and timely knowledge, if combined with faster and more flexible interorganizational transactions toward the purchase and sale of goods and services, would undoubtedly enhance our industrial productivity across nearly all sections. (p10)

Even most contributors to encyclopedias would agree that knowledge is culturally bound, structured, in part, by an individual's class, race, gender, and geographic location. But scholars' discussions about information technologies often seem to ignore the problems with knowledge claims. A keynote speaker at the 1991 University of Iowa "Symposium on Scholarly Communication: New Technologies and New Directions" talked about how the new technologies will store the data, convert it into information, and then assemble it into knowledge. He presented the technologies as data-collecting and knowledge-making machines. We need to take serious looks at what kinds of thinking and what kinds of excluding scholars are likely to be doing with the increased use of the information technologies.

As we talk about what the new information technological processes can do for scholars and students, we need also to talk about the dimensions of knowledge, including the meanings of evaluative terms such as "...perception, intuition, conceptualization, inference, representation, reflection, imagination, remembrance, conjecture, rationalization, argumentation, justification, contemplation, ratiocination, speculation, mediation, validation, [and] deliberation..." (Hawkesworth, 1989, [p551]). For example, are we increasingly more likely to call "scholarship" those research processes that use computers? We need to talk about these terms and concepts to try to distinguish between knowledge and prejudice.

Student Achievements

The third assumption is rooted in the notion that the new technologies will improve student achievement and attitudes. Any such reported successes have not been long-term, consistent, or dramatic. The reasons for this can be found, in part, by listening to what many women and men of color are saying about what is needed in the colleges and universities: diverse and creative strategies for financing education, because economic plight precludes many from beginning and completing their college educations; need for career counseling, networks, and role models, including more white women and women of color as faculty, administrators, and policymakers in all educational settings; course content more closely related to the interests and goals of white women and people of color; professors who take personal interest in women's and minorities' concerns and problems; and sensitivity to the interaction patterns of students from many race and ethnic groups. (See Carol S. Pearson, Donna L. Shavlik, and Judith G. Touchton [1989] for detailed discussions of these needs.)

Electronic Publishing

The changes in publishing technologies will bring radical changes to the concepts of intellectual property, gatekeeping, censorship, and text. Here we mention only a few of the issues that university administrators and faculty will need to address.

Already some journals are published only in electronic form, and libraries are making plans to accommodate these changes. Encyclopedias and other reference works are now available on compact discs (CD-ROM). What is seldom mentioned in pronouncements about the library of the future is that almost none of the books, journals, and reference works dealing specifically with women's issues are on CD-ROM, nor are many publishers planning to make them available in this medium.[9] The explosion of women's studies publishing in the 1970s and 1980s will have little meaning for the students of the 1990s if the valuable scholarship exists only in rare-book archives. Two WITS participants, realizing the seriousness of this situation, are planning a CD-ROM version of the *International Encyclopedia of Women's Studies* (Cheris Kramarae and Dale Spender, eds. in preparation) as a project to ensure that at least one major reference work involving international research on women will be available electronically.

9) This information was gained from recent talks with senior editors at several major publishing houses.

DIY

The University of Illinois Urbana-Champaign Senate has adopted a general education policy stating that material drawn from scholarship in various fields of inquiry on the significance of women and gender be made an integral part of a substantial number of general education courses. We will also have to convince publishers of this need (or initiate campus publishing programs), because recent studies of on-line databases show that very little of the research on women and minorities is included in existing and developing electronic databases of the humanities and social and behavioral sciences. Several national meetings have been held to discuss materials and approaches women's studies scholars use in library research, as well as the problem of access (Ellen Gay Detlefsen, 1983). Last year researchers were unable to find references to lesbian studies or information from ISIS, an important international publication on women's groups, actions, campaigns, addresses, and scholarship, on any on-line database.

If women aren't involved in the classification systems of the new electronic publishing, women will be excluded not only in the texts but also in the metatexts. As feminists have been arguing for the past two decades, culture is classification.[10] Many librarians argue that a sexist database has been established for print sources; we need to pay immediate attention to this problem as electronic databases are established. It is obvious that the changes in information technologies are having differing impacts on mainstream and on women's studies publishing.This is, of course, a very serious problem for future scholars.[11]

A related issue is the preservation of the many deteriorating books in university libraries. Present copyright law is unclear on property rights for material in electronic form; however, university library organizations are proposing legislation that allows electronic copying of library books for preservation. This copying and documenting process will cause additional pressures on already tight library budgets. Perhaps because there are relatively few books by and about women in research libraries, those books will be considered most in need of saving for future generations. However, we doubt this will be an operating rationale, and thus we ask: How will choices be made about what is copied and in what order? What is considered knowledge and scholarship has, in print history, always been gendered (Dale Spender, 1982). We mention this obvious point because university scholars have an important opportunity now to try to address, in a variety of ways, this continuing critical bias.

There are also serious problems with new books. As we are all aware, during the past decade U.S. publishing houses have been rapidly absorbed by big media conglomerates; editors are increasingly being asked to judge manuscripts not by quality but by how many truckloads of books can be sold to bookstore chains. This trend has implications for all scholars. (University presses will still publish quality books that aren't expected to sell many thousands. However, many university presses are experiencing budget cuts, along with a dwindling library market for their books.) These changes are especially serious for feminist scholars. Many of the feminist presses of the 1970s and 1980s were not purchased by the media conglomerates, and thus do not have

10) Articles on this topic appear in a number of sources including *Feminists in Science and Technology*, a publication of the Science and Technology Task Force of the National Women's Studies Association. Some of the literature in Artificial Intelligence also deals with this. (See also Mary Ellen Capek (ed.) *A Women's Thesaurus* [1987].)

11) At the University of Illinois, librarian Beth Stafford-Vaughan has been documenting the extent of this problem and suggesting ways of ensuring that women's knowledges remain a part of the library system. (See also Suzanne Damarin [1992].)

the backing to enable them to publish many books at a time or to do a great deal of advertising for the books they do publish.

Conclusion

We have sketched out some of the major problematic areas posed by the new information technologies and highlighted issues of concern for women. We have also given positive recommendations for action that can be taken to help alleviate existing inequities in terms of access, training, education, and publishing. The key areas discussed here are by no means exhaustive; rather, we chose to illuminate these four areas in order to suggest the extent to which new information technologies play a role in shaping the quality of women's academic endeavors. In addition, these areas exemplify the way in which a feminist-informed conceptualization of the impact of new information technologies can turn mainstream thought patterns upside down. That is, as we try to identify and articulate issues of gender, race, and class to the discussion of information technologies, we chart new directions for feminist scholarship at the nexus of gender and technology.

Although we have limited our comments to these four areas, other areas are just as important: for example, the need for guidelines for assessment of technologies and the need for a new ethics to guide information technology use. The importance of assessing the impact of new information technologies cannot be overstated. Unless we can agree on criteria that demonstrate the extent to which information technologies are deployed wisely, we will have little recourse when technologies run amok. In the university context, key issues include the following questions: 1) Can faculty agree on guidelines for evaluation of information technology changes? 2) Would the new technology broaden or restrict women's traditional options? 3) Would women's health be endangered? 4) Would the technology adversely affect female students and clerical workers on campus?[12] 5) Are there class and race implications associated with the technology? 6) What varying impacts are envisioned for the humanities, social sciences, and natural sciences?

12) Office design needs to be considered also, in cooperation with the women who will be placed in the offices; some university administrators have unknowingly designed work cubicles which have been nonconducive to work and have increased employee turnover.

The proliferation of new information technologies also raises important questions about computer ethics. We believe the following questions must be addressed for the ethical use of information technologies: 1) What operating values and norms will guide the use of new information technologies? 2) What key issues of responsibility and accountability are involved in the production and distribution of knowledge? 3) How are plagiarism and intellectual property handled under the new conditions? 4) Will students receive information about the ways classification schemes used in software determine reality? 5) What is to be done to lessen the increasing gulf created by the expanding use of media technology in the "First World" but not the "Third World"? We suggest it is a myth that the planet is becoming one global village serviced by common electronic communication networks; instead, the world situation is more accurately characterized by fragmentation, fracture, and competition, with each country paying attention to its own agenda and priorities.

transition
It's been this way before

We seek to make our interests explicit, and to encourage critical inspection.

We are at a crossroads; the old, familiar ways of communicating are being supplemented and replaced by new forms of electronically mediated communication. As scholars and as women, it is imperative that we take our rightful and most useful places in shaping the future forms of information technology. One of the most promising areas for the growth of women's academic communication, we believe, is in the powerful potential of computer networks. Given many women's preference for and skill in performing collaborative and cross-disciplinary research, this new medium may be well suited for our purposes. Computer networks can play a key role in fostering supportive interaction, enabling joint analyses, and providing a tool for group writing. Institutional support, however, is essential if women's voices and scholarship are to be encouraged during this time of rapid technological change. Our call to action is to insist that the development of computer networks for women be placed on the agenda of general campus discussions. University administration as well as faculty need to participate in the creation of relevant, accessible, and harassment-free information technology resources for women.

This paper has benefitted from our ongoing discussions with Dale Spender. We want to acknowledge with gratitude the insights she brought to issues of women and information technology.

References

Damarin, Suzanne (1992). "Where is Women's Knowledge in the Age of Information?" In Cheris Kramarae and Dale Spender (Eds.), *Knowledge Explosion: Generations of Feminist Scholarship*. New York: Teachers College Press.

Dertouzos, Michael L. (1991). "Communications, Computers and Networks." *Scientific American*, 265(3), 62-69.

Detlefsen, Ellen Gay (1983). "Issues of Access to Information About Women." Paper presented at the National Women's Studies Association annual conference, June 1983, Columbus, Ohio.

Estes, Nolan and Victoria Williams (1988). "Media, Information Technology, and Change." In Frederick Williams (Ed.), *Measuring the Information Society*. London: Sage.

Frenkel, Karen A. (1990). "Women and Computing." *Communications of the ACM*, 33(11), 34-46.

Hacker, Sally (1989). *Pleasure, Power, and Technology*. Boston: Unwin Hyman.

Hacker, Sally (1990). *Doing It The Hard Way: Investigations of Gender and Technology*. Boston: Unwin Hyman.

Hawkesworth, Mary E. (1989). "Knowers, Knowing, Known: Feminist Theory and Claims of Truth." *Signs: Journal of Women in Culture and Society*, 14(3), 533-557.

use them for what they are
ACCESS

that's the best part of
IT - you can DIY
no more hierarchy

Herring, Susan, Deborah Johnson, and Tamra DiBenedetto (1992). "Participation in Electronic Discourse in a 'Feminist' Field." Paper presented at the Berkeley Women and Language Conference, April 1992, University of California at Berkeley.

Kiesler, Sara, Jane Siegel, and Timothy W. McGuire (1991). "Social Psychological Aspects of Computer-Mediated Communication." In Charles Dunlop and Rob Kling (Eds.), *Computerization and Controversy: Value Conflicts and Social Choices*. Boston: Harcourt Brace Jovanovich.

Kramarae, Cheris and Paula Treichler (1990). "Power relationships in the classroom." In Susan Gabriel and Isaiah Smithson (Eds.), *Gender in the Classroom: Power and Pedagogy*. Urbana, Ill: University of Illinois Press.

Leveson, Nancy C. (1989)."Educational Pipeline Issues for Women." Information and Computer Science Department, University of California at Irvine, Irvine, Calif. (See also "Women in Computer Science" [send request to leveson@ics.uci.edu].)

Meléndez, Sara E. and Janice Petrovich (1989). "Hispanic Women Students in Higher Education: Meeting the Challenge of Diversity." In Carol S. Pearson, Donna L. Shavlik, and Judith G. Touchton (Eds.), *Educating the Majority: Women Challenge Tradition in Higher Education*. New York: Macmillan Publishing.

Pearl, Amy, Martha E. Pollack, Eve Riskin, Becky Thomas, Elizabeth Wolf, and Alice Wu. "Becoming a Computer Scientist: A Report by the ACM Committee on the Status of Women in Computing Science." *Communications of the ACM*, 33(11), 47-57.

Rakow, Lana (1988). "Gendered Technology, Gendered Practice." *Critical Studies in Mass Communication*, 5(1), 57-70.

Rakow, Lana (1992). *Gender on the Line: Women, the Telephone and Community Life*. Urbana, Ill: University of Illinois Press.

Smith, Judy (1992). "Linking Women: Computer Networks as a Feminist Resource." Presentation to Women, Information Technology and Scholarship Colloquium, March 18, 1992, Center for Advanced Study, University of Illinois.

Spender, Dale (1982). *Women of Ideas and What Men Have Done To Them*. London: Routledge.

Spender, Dale (1989). *The Writing or the Sex (or Why You Don't Have to Read Women's Writing to Know It's No Good)*. The Athene Series. New York: Pergamon.

Spender, Dale (1991). "Changes in Academic Concepts of Privacy, Originality, and Ownership of Ideas." Presentation to Women, Information Technology, and Scholarship Colloquium, October 16,1991, Center for Advanced Study, University of Illinois.

Spertus, Ellen (1992). *Why Are There So Few Women Computer Scientists?* Massachusetts Institute of Technology Artificial Intelligence Laboratory Technical Report No. 1315. Cambridge, Mass.: Massachusetts Institute of Technology Artificial Intelligence Laboratory.

Sproull, Lee (1992). "Women and the Networked Organization." Presentation to Women, Information Technology, and Scholarship Colloquium, February 12, 1992, Center for Advanced Study, University of Illinois.

Turkle, Sherry (1984). *The Second Self: Computers and the Human Spirit*. New York: Simon and Schuster.

Turkle, Sherry (1988). "Computational Reticence: Why Women Fear the Intimate Machine." In Cheris Kramarae (Ed.), *Technology and Women's Voices: Keeping in Touch*. New York: Routledge.

Turkle, Sherry and Seymour Papert (1990). "Epistemological Pluralism: Styles and Voices Within the Computer Culture." *Signs: Journal of Women in Culture and Society*, 16(1), 128-157.

Electronic Scholarship: Perform or Perish?

Dale Spender

During the 500-year reign of print, a range of scholarly conventions was developed to establish the authenticity of research, the validity of ideas, and, hence, a way of thinking about the world. But the processes of peer review – of compiling footnotes, citations, and bibliographies – designed to encourage security and a sense of trust in authority are not necessarily applicable to establishing the legitimacy of knowledge construction in the electronic media. New forms of validation are called for when research findings, thought processes, and new bodies of knowledge are published as press releases rather than in scholarly journals. Just as Ph.D. dissertations and curriculae vitae were presented in print when print was the primary medium of communication, similarly now there is pressure to move toward the electronic presentation of research, dissertations, and new forms of knowledge. This shift raises a series of fascinating issues including computer competency and copyright to ways of evaluating and thinking.

Every medium – oral, written, print, and now electronic – has its own associated thought patterns and mind sets. As we begin to use the new medium, it becomes increasingly necessary to describe and explain some of the changes that are taking place in order to appreciate their significance. For example, will the future imperative for the academic community be "Perform or perish?" What are the implications for knowledge-making, thought processes, and society in the 21st century?

"Electronic scholarship."– What does it mean? Perhaps the subtitle of this paper could well be "What's the electronic equivalent of a footnote?," "How do you get credit for messages on your e-mail?," or maybe "What's going to happen when there are no print journals, and it's all electronic?" These are all matters related to electronic scholarship, and they are not issues of the distant future, but rather issues that are currently emerging in academic institutions around the world.

Because we have developed so few conventions for evaluation of the electronic media, we face a number of problems: so many that another appropriate subtitle for this paper could be "Is the person with the bigger computer the better scholar?" In the absence of any acceptable criteria for the assessment of electronic knowledge, the answer would be in the affirmative. In the present climate, those who produce the most information have the most opportunities for gaining control, influence, and status. What needs to be addressed is whether this is satisfactory.

Although we have learned how to produce information in vast quantities, we are relatively unsophisticated when it comes to processing it. We have not developed any consistent system for sifting, refining, and evaluating the enormous amount of information we are producing. And without any way of according weight – of establishing authority or determining credibility – we are at the mercy of all forms of information manipulation. These are some of the problems that I want to examine. Like it or not, the very process of constructing, presenting, and validating knowledge is changing even as it is being produced.

Academic Knowledge and Communication

To date, research reports, theses, and academic knowledge have been presented in print, because print has been the primary medium of information. But we are moving into the electronic era, and once the electronic medium is firmly established as the primary medium of information, it is logical to expect that research reports and academic publications would be represented in the media of radio, television, video, and software. This raises questions about the presentation of the material in the new media and the effect of this presentation on the way we think about knowledge and authority.

Most academicians are aware of some of the growing pressures. In Australia, for example, the Australia Council has published the booklet *Unlocking the Academies,* which urges academicians to stop speaking to themselves, and to start speaking to the public through use of the electronic media. Many professional associations are encouraging their members to explain their research to the public. It hasn't just been various government ministers or secretaries of education in the Western world who have challenged the ivory-tower syndrome. The electronic media are exerting their own pressures.

There is understandable resistance in some academic circles. We know that traditionally, universities have been suspicious of the media. Although there may have been good grounds for the separation between academic knowledge and mass media in the past, these distinctions will be blurred in the future. Yet, if the dividing line is vanishing and the two are being brought together, how will we be able to tell the difference? And what will be the consequences?

The transition will not be without its difficulties. Once the findings of peer-reviewed research were presented in refereed journals in which credit for publication was duly given; nowadays publication is often by press release. This leads to some predictable consequences, because the process is open to all forms of exploitation. For example, the discovery of DNA was reported in *Nature* after the work had been checked and vouched for over a period of time by peers. The discovery was accredited to particular people (albeit not all the people involved, as the case study of Rosalind Franklin makes clear) and assigned a particular date of publication. These days, however, science can go public in remarkably different ways. For example, the latest promise of AIDS research or the discovery of cold fusion can be announced by press release and presented dramatically on the evening news.

Yet without benefit of peer review or time in which to ascertain the validity but this isn't a media prob- academics prob.

of findings, scientific claims made and broadcast to the world can prove to be false or deliberate hoaxes. (And the opportunity for redress can be minimal; how much has been heard about cold fusion since the dramatic announcement from Salt Lake City?) It seems that safeguards are being removed and that "the public's right to know" doesn't extend to the public's right to know what is reliable and what is false. What do these new developments do to our confidence in the knowledge presented to us daily? Who and what can we trust in the new framework of the mass media, when the dividing lines between the academic and the popular culture are being blurred?

Of course there is nothing new about the public being misled by the media, or by academicians either (see the entire body of feminist scholarship). The public has often been duped by false claims such as scientific assurances about the safety of certain products and practices. And in innumerable cases, the male-dominated academy has produced the most misleading and self-interested knowledge about women.[1]

Sometimes it is the researcher, seeking an enhanced reputation, who exploits the media in this fashion; sometimes it is the media trying to use the findings of the research community to create a good story. In either case, the boundaries between academic knowledge and mass media understandings are becoming blurred to the point that it is often difficult to know what to think or believe.

As we dismantle the dividing line between the academy and the mass media and make the shift from refereed journal to press release, we have to acknowledge that some of the old forms of protection have been lost in the process. We don't have peer review, we don't have bibliographies, footnotes and many other forms of authentication as we move from the print medium to the electronic. At the moment there is no electronic equivalent to a footnote, no way of verifying the information presented on screen or radio. Without some means of verification, we have to think of electronically communicated knowledge in ways very different from the ways of thinking about academic knowledge in the past.

Some might argue that this is how it should be, that academic knowledge in some respects has been nothing other than a commercial for the status quo over the centuries. Certainly feminists have argued that much of the knowledge produced by white men throughout history has been just as biased toward promoting the interests of the group that constructed it as any television commercial has ever been. This line of thinking would have it that, far from being a problem, the breakdown between academic knowledge and mass media knowledge – the collapse of the hierarchy of academic and popular knowledge – is a good thing.

We need to know which information is reliable and which is not. We need to be able to rank knowledge, to distinguish between reliably researched information and purely promotional presentations. We need to be able to work out the risk factor. Traditionally, academic knowledge has been accorded the status of relative reliability, partly because academicians have been

1) Examples like suggestions that women find the burden of liberation too great to bear are among the many false claims made about women. See Susan Faludi, *Backlash* (1991) for excellent exposés of how the public has been duped in this particular area.

accountable to professional associations, peers, and referees. But as these checks and balances are bypassed and become increasingly irrelevant, and as academicians go public directly in the mass media, academic knowledge could well lose its status and privileged position. Without the scholarly conventions that provide some form of imprimatur or guarantee, it might not be possible to distinguish between a televised presentation of a research report and a soap commercial.

In this postmodern world, perhaps it is preferable that academic knowledge take its place alongside knowledge produced in the mass media. Perhaps it should no longer enjoy privileged and unchallenged status but continue to be, like television commercials, scrutinized and tested for self-interest. While this could be an improvement, there are going to be numerous social and political consequences if all knowledge – whether communicated by academicians or advertisers – is unverified and enjoys comparable status. I do not want to challenge the movement from the print medium to the electronic media; I think it is as inevitable as was the shift from agriculture to industry. But I also think that ways of managing the information of the future are presenting themselves to us at this moment. These ways enhance the human condition and allow flexibility of thought and evaluation. However, to take advantage of them, we have to appreciate the fact that fundamental changes are taking place as we move from one medium to another. These changes are about the construction of knowledge, the way we think, and the way we judge. Every medium has its own associated mental patterns.

History of Information Media

Every information medium has its own associated form of social structure, and its own particular patterns of seeing the world – its own ways of thinking. So, for example, when the oral form was the primary medium of information, there were implications for everything from architecture to the sense of "here and now," and to the respect accorded the elders within the community. In an oral context, it is necessary for society to be structured around a meeting house or speakers' forum. When the only means of information distribution (speaking and listening) require direct contact, it is imperative that the whole society be designed so that people have direct access and can talk, and hear. This can give rise to small, close-knit communities; it can mean a well-developed sense of community. It can mean that those who are the repositories of the cultural values – the "stories" and meanings that are transmitted from one generation to the next – are the authorities, the people who possess knowledge and wisdom. Not surprisingly such people have considerable power, influence, and ready access to the means of distributing information.

Historically, when the *oral* was replaced by the *written* form, some very significant changes took place. First of all, changes in housing were made possible because it was no longer necessary for everyone to be in direct contact to exchange information. Words could be written down and passed around; information could be handed on to the next generation. Not only did this lead to changes in architecture, it led to changes in the way individuals thought about themselves and society. The advent of writing meant a change in the way people thought about past, present and future. Once people could live in a less communal and more dispersed fashion, notions of individuality and privacy could emerge. And once records of financial transactions, explanations, theories, instructions, and so on could be made, the very ideas about learning underwent substantial change. Questions of who and what were to be respected, what knowledge was authoritative, and who and what were reliable sources of information were markedly different from the ways of thinking and understanding that characterized the oral era.

While countless interesting intellectual developments occurred during this period, there were also some remarkable sources of resistance. Socrates, for example, raised numerous objections to the written word. He saw it as a trap that "fixed" ideas and therefore contradicted the very fundamentals of thinking. To him, what we would call "information" was dynamic and open to interrogation and negotiation, much as it was in the oral period when the speaker could be questioned by the audience and ideas could be fluid and multilayered. Because he saw writing as dangerous and diametrically opposed to mental processes, he did not commit any of his own ideas to writing. [Of course, reading about his ideas, particularly those about women and their place, one could be forgiven for suggesting that his understandings, if accurately represented by Plato, were hardly fluid enough. When it comes to his attitude to women, it could be stated without great fear of contradiction, that *he was very set in his ways.*]

But writing eventually gave way to print as the medium of information. And not only is it salutary to note some of the objections to print that were raised at its advent, it is also important to examine some of the thinking practices associated with it. Print gives a sense of order – a false sense, Socrates would claim. It has a linearity, a monodimensionality. In other words, print has a predictable and routinized pattern that has parallels in the ideas and understandings that have emerged during its reign. For example, there are many correlations between print and the scientific era that flourished while print prevailed. It is an enlightening exercise to observe the overlaps between print as a medium and science as a product. It is even more revealing to detect the ways in which the prestigious intellectual qualities of this period have been appropriated by males. Reason, rationality, detachment, and "hard data" have become associated with the superiority of the male sex. Though, as the feminist critic Adrienne Rich (1980) has suggested, such elevation of male values is clearly inaccurate; in outlining the relationship between knowledge and power she has declared that objectivity is the name that men have given to their subjectivity. Genevieve Lloyd (1984) has also demonstrated how reason and rationality are very much products of the masculine imagination.

The material nature of print has had many effects. When print first appeared on the scene, many feared the disruption it would cause. Raymond Williams (1975) has commented on records that show some people protested the manner in which print would ruin conversation in the family and lead to an anarchic society. These would be the consequences of individuals' having access to their own "private" information and of their putting it together to make sense of the world in an individualistic way, beyond the control of the authorities.

Scribes declared that this new medium of print would never catch on, that it simply wasn't possible for people to process information at such a rapid rate. Besides, everyone knew that you couldn't possibly *know* something until you had written it down.[2] Print and the mass reading and writing that were its concomitants were certainly considered dangerous by those who were in charge of the old texts [and their meanings]. So much so that in the 19th century there are actually references to a literacy crisis. But what that term meant then, as distinct from now, was that too many people were learning to write and read.

2) In a way, of course, they were right – as we know today; putting something in writing helps commit it to memory, to fixation in a way not possible in oral form; just as Socrates said–and why he had a valid objection to putting something on record.

Sometimes deliberate attempts were made to deny specific social groups access to literacy [and hence to information and ways of thinking about the world]. The working classes of England were denied this and in the United States it was a criminal offence to teach a slave to read and write. Women, of course, were systematically excluded from education after the Reformation at much the same time that print emerged as the primary medium of information. Well into the 19th century there were pronouncements from just about every branch of science and medicine that reading, writing, and thinking were dangerous for women. Articles in the *Lancet* declared that women's brains would burst and their uteruses atrophy if they engaged in any form of rigorous thinking. The famous physician J. D. Kellogg insisted that novel reading was the greatest cause of uterine disease among young women and urged parents to protect their daughters from the dreaded consequences of print.

But all these objections to the medium of print did not stop it from becoming a major force. Over the 500-year period in which print has predominated, the medium has influenced the fabric of society and the substance of thought. In the writing era, those who could read were frequently the revered members of society, the elite, the authorities who could provide information, but print disturbed the balance of power. Reading was no longer confined to select groups but was open to a mass audience. Despite the democratization of reading and the distribution of knowledge that print made possible, it is important to emphasize that new bases of power and privilege were enshrined in the medium. The old scribes, almost exclusively white and male, were replaced by the new publishers and printers who were, of course, almost exclusively white and male.

Women and the Medium

Print has been around for approximately 500 years; only relatively recently have women been influential in the medium. For four centuries and more, print has been controlled by men – a specific group of men commonly referred to as WHIMMS (White, Heterosexual, Insider, Middle-Class Men).

This male control of the medium has had enormous implications for the power structure of society, patterns of thinking, and the very high visibility of men. For most of these 500 years, the voice of women has been admitted to print only in terms acceptable to men. (This is not, of course, to suggest for a minute that women's history has not been extraordinary, or women's intellectual contribution not as creative or valuable as that of men, but to suggest that women's achievements have not been entered into men's records. For further discussion of this I can recommend – because I wrote it – a very big book, *Women of Ideas and What Men Have Done to Them* [1988a].)

Over the last three decades, however, the position of women in print has altered dramatically. During that period we have witnessed the rise of women's presses, distribution networks, bookshops, conferences, courses, and book fairs. Over the last thirty years we have seen women in more of a position to decide what will get published and what will not. Women publishers helped decide which voices will be heard and on what terms; and they have often been terms not at all acceptable to men.[3] The good news is that this "going public" has been so successful and so profitable that it has changed many of the practices of the male-controlled publishing houses. At one stage there was even discussion of the "bandwagon syndrome" in the U.K. and the U.S.: women's books were selling so well that all the mainstream publishers wanted to get on the bandwagon and put more women on their lists.

3) See, for example, *The Writing or the Sex? or Why You Don't Have to Read Women's Writing to Know It's No Good.* (Spender 1986).

But the bad news is that one reason women have been so successful with print in the last few years is that print is no longer the primary medium of information. Each year it loses more ground to the electronic media: hence the great shrinkage of mainstream publishing houses. It is a case of an area being not as important as it once was, of not being contested in the way that it had been for centuries. Women have found their way in because men are no longer defending the territory as they did in previous years. As many feminists would point out, it's another example of women being allowed into the game only to find that the goal posts have been shifted.

We are now well and truly moving into the electronic media, and it seems clear that it will probably be around 500 years – or 200 anyway – before women and other subordinate groups are able to exert any influence. It is no coincidence that the only area in which women have been able to decide what is acceptable, and what is not, is print. When it comes to the electronic media, women are not even on the horizon, let alone in positions of power and influence. There are no women's newspapers, no women's radio stations, no women's television channels, no women's film studios. (In the last few years there has been virtually only one movie that has appealed to feminist fancy –"Thelma and Louise." And even it could hardly be said to portray a politically correct or exemplary ending, yet there are so many women who are positively grateful for this production. One can only speculate on what the world and power configurations would look like if there were as many women's films, made by and for women, as there are women's books with comparable women's messages.)

but this is a reflection of power in soc, not just medium

But it's not just in the mass media and popular culture where women have little or no visibility. What is probably even more significant is that there are no women's international software companies. There are no women setting up the categories, the conventions, or the criteria for credibility in the electronic media. There are a few women working in these contexts, but they are not in decision-making positions, just as women were in publishing prior to the last thirty years, but again they were involved as those who implemented policy, not determined it.

Women, Wealth and Information

Women are as effectively excluded from the electronic media as they were from print 500 years ago. What this will do to our ways of thinking, knowing, and evaluating, what it will do for establishing who are knowers (the producers of knowledge) and who are nonknowers (the consumers or nonparticipants) is a disturbing prospect, particularly if one is female. For we know enough about knowledge and power, past and present, to predict that there will be the information-rich and the information-poor, and that the feminization of poverty will have a knowledge dimension.

So excluded are women from production in the electronic media that today's job segregation and pay differentials of the sexes will pale into insignificance compared with the job segregation and pay differentials of the 21st century. Women as a class will be among the information-poor; and there is no prize for guessing who will be in charge of what we know, how we know it, and who will to some extent be in a position to manage our thought systems. It will be the WHIMMS again.

The Electronic Era

Much has been made of the terms "postmodern" and "poststructuralist" in the last few years. And in many ways these are the appropriate terms for describing some of the new ways of looking at the world in the electronic era, because postmodern and poststructuralist are good descriptors for the electronic process. Print fixed meanings, established a linear and logical reference system, and gave a sense of order, security, certainty, and objectivity, the traditional forms of thinking and knowing in the Western world. The electronic media break these dominant patterns.

In their masculinist study of hypertext and its relationship to literary theory, George Landow and Paul Delany (1991) state that the theoretical implications of this form of electronic media "converge with some major points of contemporary literary and semiological theory, particularly with Derrida's emphasis on decentering and Barthes's conception of the readerly versus the writerly text, with post-modernism's rejection of sequential narratives and unitary perspectives, and with the issue of 'intertextuality.' In fact, hypertext creates an almost embarrassingly literal embodiment of such concepts...."(p6). With their disruption of unity, their juxtapositions, the collapse of boundaries, and the fragmentation of order, the electronic media are enabling us to reassess, make new connections, and see things differently from the way we have viewed the world through the medium of print. We have entered a new phase, yet there are few signposts to guide the way.

With the changes in media come significant changes in social practice. Print gave the masses access to reading, and now the electronic media give an increasing number of people access to "authoring." (This assumes access to a computer, of course.) As the 19th century romantic image of the solitary male artist in the garret, inspired by the muse, is giving way to the image of a team of production writers for television or of authors of software, we are witnessing the death of the writer.

Looking back to the introduction of print and the rise of a mass readership, we can see that the changes that took place could be considered the deprofessionalization of the reader or the democratization of knowledge. Depending on the standpoint, similar distinctions could be made with the introduction of the electronic media. Now that so many people can become authors (including the makers of amateur videos, who can record violence, massacres, and riots and whose work can be screened around the world on the evening news), are we witnessing the deprofessionalization of the author, or the democratization of knowledge?

Whose Information?

These broad political and social evaluations are not the only ones we have to take into consideration; there is also the issue of the reliability of the information produced. When so many people, with so many competing vested interests, can make so much information, what can we trust? At one end of the spectrum is the position of not trusting anything – "absolute relativism" and the belief that there are as many truths as there are makers. At the other end is the acceptance that comes with the assumption that what's on the screen, on the news, on the software program, has to be TRUE. So the film "JFK," for example, becomes the real story of the assassination of President Kennedy for many people; so the beautifully presented television commercial on the way Exxon claims to have cleaned up Alaska becomes the truth in many people's minds about the current state of the environment.

Susan Faludi's *Backlash* (1991) is a remarkable achievement because she takes on the way in which certain media truths and cultural narratives (in this case, those directed toward undermining women) are constructed in defiance of the evidence. In doing this she makes a strong case for the need for evaluative criteria. Unless and until we address the crucial issue of the status and accountability of various forms of information in an information-driven society, we are more likely to be unwittingly shaped by the emerging media than to be in a position to shape processes and evaluate credibility. And this is particularly the case as the boundaries between academic knowledge and commercials weaken and collapse.

That literally hundreds of issues could be addressed in this context gives us some idea of the extent of the conversion process we are involved in. Some examples include ideas about intellectual property, copyright, the place of the writer, or even the role and place of the academician in the 21st century.

From Page to Performance

Performance, as compared with print, has implications for the writer in general (as well as the academic author). The majority of the women whose work was included in *Heroines*, an anthology of contemporary Australian women's writing, earned more from the performance of their work than they did from the printing of it. (Publishers, in selecting titles, now want to know whether the author is promotable and can perform the work.) The pressure to perform is there right across the board; and in performance a range of problems demand attention. Some of them are proving to be quite amusing. Perhaps.

What will it mean if academicians have to perform in the electronic media to get a reputation and to get credit for the publication of their research? Just as it was essential to publish in print when print was the primary medium of information, why should it not be essential to "publish" in the electronic form when it is unchallenged as the primary medium of information? What are the implications for mumbling, shifty-eyed academics whose very presentation of their work would – like Richard Nixon's "five-o'clock shadow"– undermine the credibility of their research? And if academicians cannot satisfactorily perform their own work, should they hire someone else to perform it for them, just as those who could not write convincingly (or who could not write at all) hired scribes to represent their ideas in the Middle Ages?

If the work is not performed, will it be deemed unpublished? It is not at all difficult to see how "publish or perish" could soon become "perform or perish." We are certainly reaching the stage at which it is not enough to write a book or do the research – the work has to be performed. And performance isn't just confined to going public with the work; it can also reach into the very processes of research itself.

Action-based research, for example, shows how performance is making its presence felt; and our methods are changing as market research and academic research are merging.[4] Reared as I have been with print, my research has often consisted of interrogating particular texts. I have critiqued premises, arguments, and presentations and worked exclusively with words. But a new mode of research is evolving where the researcher interrogates not just the text–but the author. The book *Backlash* (Faludi, 1991) provides some excellent examples of this process. The author went to a producer of particular information and examined (often with wonderful results) the material context in which the information was generated. Susan Faludi questioned the female author of many of Ronald Reagan's policies on women's place in the home – only to find a public and powerful woman who had left her husband in another state looking after the kids and who was quite clear that she had the better part of the bargain. But to keep her desired life-style she argued daily that the well-being of the nation depended on women's performing their domestic duties. Needless to say, it was not necessary for Susan Faludi to

4) One of my current survey questions is: If you wanted to build a power station, would you hire a public relations person or an engineer to begin the research? The responses are very interesting.

critique the printed text to demonstrate the falseness of the position in these circumstances.

Intellectual Property

What do the electronic media mean in relation to that sacred tenet, the ownership of ideas? What is the electronic equivalent to the footnote? Intellectual property is currently a minefield; already in television and film it is impossible to designate an owner or author when teams are working on the script.

Although these are all most interesting issues, I want to concentrate on a more mundane aspect of the problem of intellectual property – that of the conventions of scholarship. My point in doing this is to illustrate some of the issues we face in moving from one medium to another and the implications the shift has for power and for thinking. Not that I have any of the solutions, of course; but it is important to raise the questions and make the area a topic.

If we want to distinguish academic knowledge from a commercial, or a soap opera, or a public-relations presentation – of course, wanting to do so assumes a hierarchy of knowledge with which many might want to quarrel in this postmodern era – it is necessary for us to develop some guidelines for the authentication of knowledge. Now at this stage I am not passing judgment on whether or not we want academic knowledge (though as a feminist there is much I could throw away without a second thought); academic knowledge is part of the contemporary scene. It is still a very powerful force (although not nearly as influential as when print was the primary medium), and as such, I want academic knowledge to be accountable in some way.

Given that the electronic era is here to stay, and that universities are likely to be around for quite a while, producing privileged knowledge, I want to be able to do a little consumer testing; I want to have some idea about the claims and the substance of what is being produced in the academic community. This means developing criteria of credibility for the electronic media. It means making clear the form, the expectations, and the rules for evaluation. I want ways of checking to be developed, rather than for the topic to be ignored. And as a feminist, I am most concerned that women should have a say in what these conventions should be. I don't want a repeat performance of men's convenient construction of objectivity and their appropriation of it as proof of their own superior intellectuality. There's real power in the practices that we can set up, and I have a vested interest in ensuring that equity prevails.

There are numerous starting places for exploring this topic, so I am going to describe a specific task within the academic framework. For the last few months, I have been part of a working party looking at the presentation of research degrees as videos and as software, and I will summarize here some of the thorny issues that arise as we make the transformation from print to the electronic media. I am not going to address the relative merits of video and print, or question whether things can be done in video that cannot be done in print; I think that in many situations video is the better medium, although I think students should be able to make this case for themselves. Use of videos is not a scenario of the distant future; a master's thesis has already been presented as a video at Waikato University, and in the U.S. the practice is becoming increasingly common. These are not cases of a video being used as an accompaniment or an illustration for part of a dissertation, but of the dissertation, itself, being electronic.

Some of the requirements for presenting a Ph.D. dissertation as a video are:

1. Competency with the medium
It can reasonably be assumed that a student is proficient at writing and reading by the time he or she reaches postgraduate status. Many of the previous qualifications for this status have been designed to test for literacy and competency, and although the writing ability of some Ph.D. students is open to question, a certain level of proficiency can be taken for granted. But this is not the case with video competency. If students want to present an electronic dissertation, should proof of video proficiency be required? If so, by whom and to what standards? Would the media departments of universities take responsibility for competency in the medium in much the same way English departments take responsibility for literacy? What are the implications of this for the student, the academic disciplines, the university – and our ways of thinking?

2. Relationship with the media department
Does the student produce the video alone, or with the media department of a university? We would not think it appropriate for students working with print to hand over their work to a "publisher" who would write it up for them, (although we certainly think it permissible to have a Ph.D. dissertation typed by a professional). We don't insist that the form be entirely the student's own work. So how would we feel about research students handing over their data to video professionals who would write it up for them? And what is the role of students in a video production? Are they the interviewers, presenters, editors, or scriptwriters? Are they the technicians and camerapersons? Do the students provide the intellectual content and the media department do all the hands-on work? How can viewers tell what is what in these circumstances? How professional does the product have to be? Are home videos, for example, of sufficient standard? Again, we can make some comparisons with the print Ph.D. dissertation; we certainly wouldn't accept a handwritten dissertation, and perhaps we should not accept a home video standard for a research degree. These are only some of the preliminary questions.

3. Supervision
What does the concept of supervision mean when a Ph.D. dissertation is presented on video? Could it be that not only will old academicians have to learn new tricks to perform their own work, they will have to learn how to supervise students who want to present their information in the new primary form? Perhaps we will see the beginning of joint supervisions, by an academician and an audiovisual technician. And what will be supervised anyway? Content or form? Medium or message? Quality of ideas or of representation?

4. Audience

Who is the video for? Is the audience the examiners, as it was with the print dissertation or is it assumed that the audience is much wider – even commercial? It has been argued that one reason for doing an electronic dissertation is that it can reach a wider audience. The grounds for presenting a dissertation as a video at Waikato were that the Maori woman who presented it wanted to be able to give back to the community she studied the information with which they had provided her and which they could use. To feed back the research to those being researched seems a justifiable motive, but it means that the examiners are by no means the only audience, and this has significant implications. Of course, the students presenting electronic dissertations may be in exactly the same position as many who have presented them in print in recent years, who have done one version for the examiners and another, a rewrite, for commercial publication as a book.

5. Ownership

Who will own the video when it is completed – the media department or television unit that supplied the equipment, personnel, and facilities? Who can sell or distribute the video? Who pays? What about funding? As in the real world, what if the video is a cooperative or team effort? How will copyright be assigned, and how will degrees be given? What are the opportunities here for exploitation? I don't just mean whose view of the world (the student's or the media department's) will prevail. You don't have to be a feminist to work out that when it comes to technology, boys get the equipment and girls get to clean up. And you don't have to be a media expert to ask what is the meaning of a cheap versus an expensive production.

6. Raw footage as data

What is the role of raw footage of video dissertations? Should it be kept as the raw data in the same way that it has been customary to keep the raw data not included in a print dissertation? Or does the raw footage assume the same status as "drafts"? We do not require students presenting dissertations in print to keep all the drafts of their final product; however, keeping video drafts may be necessary so we can check what the student has left out of the product. If so, what about balance, bias, and comprehensive coverage? Might there be occasions when students are asked to supply raw footage, and then are disqualified on the grounds that they distorted their final results? Keeping all the footage that has been filmed also raises the questions of where to keep it, how to file it, and how to use it.

7. Writing a script

No student could produce a video without first writing a script, even if it is like a shopping list: "get this," "do that," "follow up with," etc. But does this list become part of the project? Is writing it a stage in the process of doing an electronic dissertation? If so, who critiques it? Who accredits it? Does the script become part of the final product on which the student is assessed?

8. Data gathering
How are data gathered and what are the issues involved, particularly in relation to privacy? If a video is being made about sexual abuse of children, or some aspect of Aboriginal life, or even with person-on-the-street interviews, what rights do the objects of the research have? Are their faces blocked out? What sort of permissions should be signed? Who draws up and administers such a system?

9. Distribution
Will the video gather dust on the library shelves as many a print dissertation has? Or will the new form be in demand in a way that the old has not? Can students stipulate that the video be on restricted use, that it be for academic purposes only? Or will the library and media department be able to distribute all or sell part, and thereby recoup some of the costs? If it has commercial potential, who decides what can be sold? And what opportunity for constructing new (and unaccountable) truths in this context?

10. Methodology
All of the above considerations can make a difference in the way material is gathered and in how it is used and assessed. For example, the greater the degree of privacy, the more frank the respondents and interviewees might be – the more intimate the issues that may be pursued. Questions about how, when, and why decisions are made make a good case for a student's keeping a journal that documents progress, justifies perspectives, and acknowledges bias. This journal might even become part of the dissertation.

Of course, all these issues beg the question of the criteria that are going to be used to gauge academic excellence. It might even be the case that academic excellence is not an appropriate concept in the knowledge construction of the 21st century. Are there going to be standards for originality, contribution to the discipline, quality of presentation, etc.? And what will be the electronic equivalent of the footnote? How can references be provided in this context? Will footnotes, citations, and so on be provided as subtitles, or will students face the camera at the end of the video and read the bibliography, providing the annotations of what was used when and where – and with what effect? Or will fact sheets be distributed in much the same way radio and television broadcasting authorities provide further information, upon request, for authentication and checking after a program has been aired? Or does all this come as credits at the beginning?

A New Beginning

What are the implications of all these new processes, insights, and developments of conventions for our own thinking? What happens as we – raised on print – make the shift to electronic patterns of thinking? So many issues are raised as we enter the information revolution, and the major concern I have is that we don't seem to want to be aware of our own process. We don't seem to want to monitor what is happening, or to be alert to the huge potential for the misuse of power.

We are probably a unique group in that we are involved in this transition process. Dinosaurs or divergent thinkers? – Who knows what we are at the moment? In either case, I suspect it is unlikely that there will be another generation that is as thoroughly comfortable with print as we are, and this in itself bears thinking about. Not that I believe print will entirely disappear. There is no evidence that a new information medium has eliminated an older one; we still use oral, written, and print media, though their roles and significance have changed. Perhaps the change in information technology is parallel to that in photography – black-and-white film is still available, though less accessible now that we have color photography. Perhaps once print is no longer the primary medium of information it will be more available for artistic and creative use, like black-and-white photographs are.

What I know is that we are going to have a few headaches in our generation as we make the transition. And, what I know is that when it comes to subordinated groups, our knowledge is almost exclusively encoded in the medium of print, and therefore is very much at risk. Feminists of my generation often complain that younger women know next to nothing about feminist theory and history, and they assume that this is somehow the fault of the younger women. But as far as I am concerned, the problem is that in all the sources to which the next generation goes for information, feminism simply isn't there. It isn't in girls' or women's magazines or in film, video, television, or software. And for me, this problem is much of what electronic scholarship is about and why an enormous amount of work remains to be done.

I suspect that women's knowledge, scholarship, and ways of thinking are threatened now more than at any other time, and I believe that the changes in the medium of information, and the exclusion of women from its production, are going to have profound consequences for society, power and gender, the construction of academic knowledge, and our ways of seeing the world. If there is any question that needs to be raised about electronic scholarship in the 21st century, it is about thought and manipulation. It is about knowledge and power.

References

Australia Council (n.d.). *Unlocking the Academies.* (Discussion paper and proposals for action, from Forum I, following the National Ideas Summit, February 26, 1990)

Faludi, Susan (1991). *Backlash.* New York: Crown.

Landow, George and Paul Delany (1991). "Hypertext, Hypermedia and Literary Studies: The State of the Art" in Paul Delany and George Landow, (Eds.), *Hypermedia and Literary Studies.* Cambridge, Mass.: Massachusetts Institute of Technology Press, 3-50.

Lloyd, Genevieve (1984). *The Man of Reason: "Male" and "Female" in Western Philosophy.* London: Methuen.

Rich, Adrienne (1980). *On Lies, Secrets and Silence.* Virago: London.
Spender, Dale (1988a). *Women of Ideas and What Men Have Done to Them.* London: Pandora/Harper-Collins.
Spender, Dale (1988b). *The Writing or the Sex – Or Why You Don't Have to Read Women's Writing to Know It's No Good.* New York: Athene, Teachers College Press.
Spender, Dale (Ed.) (1991). *Heroines: A Contemporary Anthology of Australian Women Writers.* Australia: Penguin.
Williams, Raymond (1975). *The Long Revolution.* Middlesex: Penguin.

Networked Serials, Scholarly Publishing, and Electronic Resource Sharing in Academic Libraries: A Dilemma of Ownership

Ann L. Okerson

The Current "Crisis" Situation in Academic Publishing

Librarians speak of the current crisis in academic publishing, referring to such interconnected problems as:

- *the high prices of scientific and technical monographs and journals*
- *the high volume of academic literature, much of which remains unread either because there is so much of it or because of its quality*
- *the slowness of relevant materials to appear in print distribution, slower than the researchers would wish and slower than the current pace of scientific growth seems to demand*

The constituents of the "information chain"– authors, editors, publishers, libraries, and readers – increasingly look to electronic publishing, and in particular publishing and distribution via the electronic networks, as a solution to many of these problems; that is, as a way in which speed of production and access can be measurably improved, information can be stored and purchased more cost-effectively, and, in at least the midterm, prices can be contained or reduced. Because the electronic networks are currently publicly and academically subsidized and most of the scholarly communication on them is created by the not-for-profit sector (e.g., academicians and researchers), scholars and librarians are hoping that information might flow more freely in the networked world to come than it currently does on paper, and that it will be a great deal easier to own materials collectively and share them between libraries (and researchers) than at present.

This paper is based on work done for the North Carolina Research Libraries and the Scholarly Communications Committee of the Association of Research Libraries.

A closer look at publishing practices and the way they are translating into the electronic arena suggests, however, that this vision could be little more than wishful thinking. The fundamental issue in regard to holding and sharing information resources in the electronic environment, as it turns out, may be one not so much of technology as of ownership. And, interestingly, the question of ownership is one of those that already vexes today, particularly with paper publication formats and for similar reasons.

The Effect of Copyright Transfer on an Author's Ownership/Control of the Work in the U.S.

By tradition, in the process of scholarly publishing, effective "ownership" (that is, control) of writings usually passes from the hands of the creators/authors/scholars to publishers through the act of copyright assignment. The copyright transfer the author signs when an article is accepted for publication accomplishes two objectives that (for the most part) are entwined, although this is not necessarily the case.

First, the author (or authors) attests that the written work is appropriately original and thus can be legally assigned. This indemnifies the publisher against any potential plagiarism accusations or related actions.

Second, the author gives control of the printed form of the work to the publisher, who thus becomes its new "owner." This ownership, which is valid for the duration of copyright (the lifetime of the author plus fifty years), allows the new owner to sell or resell the information as is deemed reasonable and in a way the market will support. In other words, copyright provides the legal framework for ownership transfer and privitization of an author's work.

For the most part, the current copyright transfer forms are quite comprehensive. They give the publisher the rights to produce the work in paper, in microform, in new technological formats, and, as some contracts specify, in any form not yet created but that may be created. The author generally retains the right to ask the publisher's permission to reproduce the work as part of another work, such as a book or a compilation. The practice is that normally the publisher will grant such permission provided the original source is credited. Additionally, the author is often supplied with preprints or offprints for private distribution. Any other distribution by the author must fall within the "fair use" provision of the Copyright Act of the United States.

Who the publisher-owner is has had an enormous impact on the prices charged and the rights allowed to the customer. According to a number of cost-per-unit studies of various kinds of STM (scientific, technical, medical) journal pricing, the not-for-profit producers (such as university presses and learned societies) consistently sell information at prices anywhere from two to twenty times less than the for-profit or commercial publishers. There may be understandable reasons for such differentials but the point is that, in fact, the situation does exist. The publishing process has evolved into a contractual exchange in which authors give up ownership in return for the editing and distribution of the work. "Validation" in the form of peer review is built into the publishing process, although peer review continues to be interjected by the academy as a nonremunerative process (thus reducing publication costs), in contrast to the normal practices of commercial publishers.

Especially with regard to periodical articles, the author's reward is usually in the form of recognition of the work rather than in direct compensation from the publisher or in royalties. In fact, under the current publishing system, offering such compensation to authors could be counterproductive. First, only a minority of articles are copied often enough that royalties would accrue. Second, direct remuneration to authors would conceivably raise the price of academic writings to even less affordable levels and would exacerbate the current pricing situation. It can therefore be argued that both author and publisher are compensated in ways that matter to them. Nonetheless, the creator loses ownership of the work, and in the past decade or so, libraries are finding it increasingly difficult to afford repurchase.

The "Rights" of Print-on-Paper Purchasers

In the current print-on-paper tradition, some rights accrue to purchasers of published writings, that is, those who acquire (and thus own) a copy of the author's printed artifact. Whether individuals or libraries, these new owners have considerable latitude in what they do with the material: they may organize it, lend it as they choose (even ship the physical item around the world to outside borrowers), and in the end, when they are good and tired of it, they may throw the physical item away or sell it at a garage sale.

The one limitation – and it is considerable – on acquirers of the paper artifact has to do with copying or reproducing the items or parts of the items. Restraints have been placed on purchasers largely in order to protect the livelihood of the publishers who take the production risk. In the light of the publishers' risk, which can be considerable, it is useful to bear in mind (again) that in scholarly publishing the original authors of the work, particularly authors of articles in journals, are financially uncompensated, as are, for the most part, the editorial board members and the peer reviewers. Authors often seem to believe that they have some special sharing and distributing privileges for the writing they create, but in fact they have (except for their clutch of offprints) no more rights to copy the work than libraries or any other purchasers.

"Fair Use"

The restraints upon purchasers of copyrighted materials are outlined in the "fair use" provisions of the 1976 Copyright Act of the United States. The Act gives special dispensations to users for educational and not-for-profit purposes but nonetheless restricts reproduction and replication (as opposed to handling of the purchased item itself). To determine if use is "fair," the following questions are asked:

- *Is the reproduction for profit (resale) or not for profit?*
- *If not for profit, could the number of copies made affect the publisher/owner's revenue stream?*
- *What proportion of the work is copied?*
- *How often is it copied?*

The guidelines to the 1976 Copyright Act further suggest that a library ought not to request (on interlibrary loan) more than five articles a year out of any journal title. Of course, because these are guidelines only, libraries may choose to apply them with liberal interpretations and procure for free more than five articles in a given year. For a quarterly publication, five articles might not be unreasonable, but for expensive and voluminous titles producing hundreds of articles a year at subscription prices of hundreds or thousands of dollars per year, five is far from realistic and impedes the ability to share resources among institutions.

More than the five guideline copies can be made in a year provided that either the publisher or the publisher's collection agency (such as the Copyright Clearance Center) is reimbursed. It is in the copying of more than five articles in any given year out of any given journal title that paper restrictions begin to resemble those in the emerging marketplace and the current publisher/distributor practice for electronic counterparts of original publications.

CD-ROM Prices as a Barometer of Electronic Models and Prices to Come

As a way station to electronic network distribution, consider the current model prevailing for the "static" electronic CD-ROM (compact disc-read-only memory). Because they share with networked products the potential for easy, wide, quick, and somewhat undisciplined copying and sharing, most CD-ROM products are licensed rather than sold. The license gives the CD-ROM to a library for the duration of the agreement, often a year for a subscription. Such signed contracts take precedence over laws and the library or other signee is required to adhere to what has been promised in the license.

Commonly, such licenses may

- *require that the CD disk be returned if the subscription is cancelled*
- *limit how many stations are linked and how many users can use the disk at a time*
- *prohibit sharing with nonmembers of the subscriber institution*

With the CD-ROM products, the library's or individual purchaser's right to share is defined and limited by the wording of the license. In the license model, the library is no longer an owner of even a copy of a physical artifact, as it was in paper, although there is still a physical artifact.

Ownership of Electronic Information

Print-on-paper publishers are positioning themselves to publish on electronic networks. In networked distribution, there is no precise product such as an iridescent disk, let alone a paper artifact. What can be supplied to the purchaser is the information itself, delivered to the library or user over a network as a pattern of electronic impulses. These may be read by the end-user at a screen, printed by that user on a printer, or accessed by the library on behalf of a current or anticipated request. Furthermore, the responsibility for any actual printing or rendering into paper form for the user is passed on to the licensee, so the obligations of the publisher-owner are somewhat diminished or at least altered. In fact, it is questionable whether the publisher can any longer guarantee to provide the integrity-authenticity component of "value added" that is possible more reliably on paper – it is much more difficult electronically to ensure that a printed iteration of the transmitted document (not to mention an electronic copy) is accurate or even honest. Not that these problems do not exist with xeroxing or otherwise copying paper documents, but electronically the problems and opportunities can be accelerated and exacerbated.

Some Scenarios by Which Libraries Will Access Electronic Networked Information

1. Local subscription (site license).
Libraries may choose to purchase the information (such as a journal or a database) for loading into a local system (mainframe computer or CDs, linked to additional workstations both in the building and through the user community). A precedent has already been set for charging for electronic information considerably more than for information on paper. Licenses are often based on potential number of users or number of users who have access at any given moment. The publisher has usually either developed searching or other software or contracted that responsibility to a specialist intermediary, and those costs and the desired related profits are part of the cost of the product. Currently, commercial CD-ROM prices are very high. Four reasons for such pricing might be postulated:

First, the necessary development in a new and dynamic technical environment with very few standards can be costly. Second, value to the user is added (e.g., ubiquitousness, speed, searchability). Third, publishers and libraries are accustomed to the subscription model in which monies are collected up front for the year in advance. Fourth, customers appear willing to pay.

2. Resource sharing (multisite license).
The library, a consortium of libraries, or a library utility may elect to become a broad-based distributor for an electronic journal or database or product. In such a case, other libraries may obtain the information from this organization on an agreed-upon basis. The distributing library has a broader (more comprehensive and more expensive) license from the publisher and still does not own the information it distributes. Outside users may gain access for a fee. The economic risks are shared by both the publisher and the distributor.

3. Access (pay "by the drink").
The publisher or a commercial intermediary controls and distributes electronic information, often by means of on-line connections.This offers the option of a great deal of service with less worry, at probably the highest price of all the options. In this model, as indeed in all those outlined here, no resource sharing as we have known it is possible. Libraries share only out-of-date, aging, dusty books, because increasingly libraries neither own nor control any information except for those materials bought long ago in the 1990s.

4. Publishing by the library, scholar, university, or learned society.
A rare instance of this scenario is the positioning of the Online Computer Library Center library service (through its partnership with American Association of Advancement in Science on the proposed Clinical Trials electronic journal) as an electronic publisher. In this case, the user community is an important partner in fixing subscription prices and access. Informal exam-

ples are the papers, files, documents, and lists on the network today and accessible by file transfer protocol (ftp) or by subscription.

A world of electronic distribution, with no physical artifacts to "own," alters all notions of what libraries are about and how they work as a centralized function, given the assumption that within twenty years much of what scholars want to read will be accessible quickly and conveniently in the networked format at the individual researcher's desktop. All these communication changes will happen. It is only a question of when, what the expense will be, and filling in the detail.

Some Initiatives to Retain Scholarly Ownership and Access to Creative Scholarly Work

If colleges, universities, and libraries are to be safe harbors for growth of ideas and for building on knowledge, a critical focus must be to ensure that ownership of information rests, at least to some extent, in scholars' hands. What are some of the ways in which the academic institution might address and ensure ownership of (and thus ability to share) its own creations? There are several possibilities, and the following list is by no means exhaustive.

1. Support and fund learned societies and university presses as publishers, in both paper and electronic formats.

2. Encourage authors to write for academic (i.e., university and learned society) presses and outlets. Scholars should seek publishers with a common mission and a track record of affordability and responsiveness. Provide editorial services for such publishers.

3. Encourage creators to read copyright statements sent to them for signature and to attempt to retain some rights (e.g., for electronic distribution) for themselves and their institutions. The chances of effecting changes in publication policy depends on the creators of material showing awareness and concern about this emerging new situation.

4. Universities (academic authors and the administration), and preferably groups of universities in local consortia or in associations (the National Association of State, University and Land Grant Colleges or the American Association of Universities, for example), should develop model copyright transfer forms for their authors to sign. These forms might retain some ownership for the authors' institution, particularly in electronic distribution, or more favorable license terms for the institution or consortium.

5. Develop a university and library negotiating model for site licenses that are desirable and affordable to these institutions. Current pricing for such publications appears to the library community to be unacceptably high and even less affordable than paper output, while quality is often questionable and software is nonstandard and proprietary. Indeed, the desirability of vendors packaging the data with (often very expensive) special software deserves close evaluation – the software may not always enhance the usability of the data.

6. The Association of Research Libraries and higher education organizations should work with the appropriate government agencies and officials to extend article 105 of the Copyright Act (which provides that work done by federal government employees on government time be exempt from copyright; this article makes such work freely shareable) to work done with government funds, such as grants and contracts with such tax-supported agencies as the National Endowment for the Humanities, the National Institutes of Health, the National Science Foundation, the Department of Education, and others.

7. Scholars creating and placing information on the network ought to attach a statement to their work that clearly expresses their wishes for its use. There is a generous, frontiering spirit about the Net that lets anything be reproduced by almost anyone. As more and more substantive work is deposited on the Net, it can be downloaded and even printed for sale. This is the time for every list, e-journal, file, and article to include appropriate statements about ownership. For example, Michael Strangelove and Diane Kovacs' electronic dictionaries clearly allow electronic transfer for not-for-profit purposes but no full-paper download without express permission.The Bryn Mawr Classical Review allows no reproduction beyond "fair use" without permission of the editors.

8. The Net and its tens of thousands of items is a wondrous source. It is as uncharted as the Amazonian jungles. We need to be able to see the trees for the forest, and it is time that learned societies began developing not only good indexing to paper literature but also indexing to network sources and files. It is not too soon to begin such maps. Placing one's work on the Net is not very rewarding if it cannot be found or recognized. Proper indexing is one way of achieving respectability for authored works deposited on academic networks rather than in a more conventional paper outlet.

9. The Net would be a fine place to begin various semiformal preprint series for works that are intended to appear later in more traditional forms such as journals. Eventually one could add peer review on the Net and bypass the longer publication process, if that proves useful. We need leadership in such initiatives from the learned societies.

10. List owners and journal editors could seek official partnerships, sanctions, or institutionalization for their works. Otherwise, as the Net begins to cost individual users money–and for various reasons it will – good publications will be vulnerable financially. Institutions are more stable than individuals and outlast them. The earliest journals begun by individuals generally lasted only a few issues before fading. The institutional titles tended to survive.

11. Works currently under copyright cannot easily be put into the public domain. The future of information for academic institutions can, however, be optimized through actions scholars take from today forward to maintain ownership and access.

12. We must engage in thoughtful discussions and seek useful outcomes for delivering and sharing networked information. The new medium offers many opportunities (and presents many vexing problems) for a brand-new conception of what scholarly communication can be. Current discussions postulate "intelligent documents," interactive and collaborative writing, and continuing dialogue about ideas and articles, which are not necessarily the last word on any subject. Writings are available from preprint to revision to "final" to continuously annotated form. The philosophical concept of "living documents" represents a fundamental change from the fixed archival version that is encouraged by the paper format. Would today's publisher commit to supporting the continuing development of an idea after fixing and licensing an electronic version? Who will develop the mechanisms to link together related articles in different electronic journals, a linkage that clearly will be needed and will affect the nature of electronic documents and their authorship, ownership, and control?

To a large extent, the future is in the hands of the scholars. A good future demands our best energies and active partnerships between scholars, learned societies, universities, and libraries whose mission is access to the body of knowledge for future generations.

Women and Men on Electronic Networks: A Conversation or a Monologue?

Cheris Kramarae
H. Jeanie Taylor

The promises of the new technologies are enticing: Electronic networks provide low-cost communication systems that enable an increasing number of people (in the wealthier countries) who have access to them to cross barriers of space, time, and social categories. These popular networks use computer tools and long-distance telecommunication lines to provide high-speed information exchange, linking individuals and groups. The examples of the benefits to many people using the networks are growing.[1]

For example, women and other marginalized people in many places and occupations are using the electronic networks to maintain easy, quick connections to kindred souls with shared interests, nearby or far away. Rural students and teachers in the U.S. state of Montana are linking their computerized bulletin board and electronic mail system (called Big Sky Telegraph) with Internet, an international computer networking service, enabling these people, at least theoretically, to communicate and share ideas with thousands of communities all over the world. Judy Smith, project director of the Women's Opportunity and Resource Development (WORD) center in Missoula, Montana, uses Big Sky Telegraph to "message" other women's centers and coordinates efforts to attend key legislative meetings (Evan Brown, 1991). Women participating in the Women's Studies network are exchanging concerns, information, and action suggestions. SeniorNet, a small research project in the U.S., has provided the opportunity for at least a few elders to "talk"[2] across geographical areas about such topics as health and fitness, gardening, and recreation (Richard Adler, 1988). In 1989 students from China studying abroad used computer bulletin boards and electronic mail to share their worries, anger, and information about the revolution and the efforts to suppress it in their homeland.

In general, these networks are available to people who work for organizations with investments in computers and their promises.[3] Lee Sproull and Sara Kiesler report that these new forms of communication are changing the ways that large organizations in the "Western" countries function–increasing, they argue, a democratic free exchange of information (Lee Sproull and Sarah Kiesler, 1991, p13).

If people's uses of these networks are indeed bringing about major changes

1) A woman from Estonia points out that this discussion presumes that users live in a democracy where people basically consider access to the nets a right or privilege. In some societies network use could become a requirement or duty, and could be used to separate people rather than link them.

2) Participants at the Gender, Technology and Ethics conference, held on June 1-3, 1992, in Lulea, Sweden, where a version of this paper was presented, pointed out that using talk terminology may affect the way we conceptualize words on the network. Judy Smith and Ellen Balka (1988) use the term "chatting," and do not reread or rewrite to correct spelling or grammar errors in their messages, to deliberately maintain an informality that invites people of many educational levels and interests to enter into a discussion.

3) We are focusing on seemingly volunteer uses of networks. Of course, in many organizations electronic networks are used to distribute company messages and employees are required to read them.

in organizations, we are particularly interested that women and other marginalized people are included in the conversations about, and on, the nets. We are already seeing problems, including sexual harassment, that work against that equal exchange for all promised by so many of the experts.

Here, we focus on what is happening in the universities, organizations that have a particular interest in freedom of speech, openness, innovation, and the free exchange of ideas. Universities may have more of a chance to institute change "at home" and thus to influence change in the larger world. Many other large organizations have a greater stake in encouraging a common corporate voice – and thus more interest in silencing dissension in the ranks. We focus on the university because that is where we have experience and because universities could set an example not only for dealing with abusive behavior on the networks but also encouraging inclusive and collaborative communication. The concerns we have about computers and educational settings are many. For example, elsewhere Cheris Kramarae (1989) has documented the mismatch between the types of educational problems that computer software companies propose to correct and the types of problems which are given attention by women and "minorities". Here, we focus on problems women are experiencing on electronic networks, and suggest some guidelines to help minimize the problems for women and "minorities" on the nets.[4]

Increasingly, universities will be judged by whether they have state-of-the-art computing equipment to support staff, students, and faculty work. Increasingly, universities will be judged by how they use this equipment. This report suggests some ways to avoid the misuse and abuse of the new electronic technologies that are transforming universities but often forming patterns that replicate or intensify previous problems. While we write here only about the networks that are used daily by millions of faculty, staff, and students on campuses across the nation (and around the world), we, along with the other participants of the Women, Information Technology and Scholarship (WITS) colloquium at the University of Illinois,[5] have related concerns about the uses of computers in classroom and in libraries.

4) A few of the problems are also being addressed by the Ethics Case Studies, sponsored by Educational Uses of Information Technology, a program of EDUCOM, a consortium of more than 600 colleges and universities concerned about ethics in computing. The director of the Ethics study is Sarah P. Webster, assistant professor of computer applications at the State University of New York College of Environmental Science and Forestry. She says that ethical problems reported range from "students using a computer network to threaten or harass someone, to a department chairman's ordering faculty members to participate in software theft, to university officials' breaking into professors' computer files" (David L. Wilson, 1991).

5) WITS is a faculty and administration colloquium, meeting two or three times a month, sponsored by the Center for Advanced Study at the University of Illinois at Urbana-Champaign. Cheris Kramarae and Jeanie Taylor are co-organizers of the colloquium. Maureen Ebben is the research assistant for the project.

The Settings for the New Technologies

The resistance of most universities to change what has been characterized as a "chilly climate" for women and minorities is well documented (Roberta Hall and Bernice Sandler, 1982). After several decades of feminist documentation and explanation, even *The New York Times* has recognized, in a front page story, that bias against girls is "rife" in schools, resulting in "lasting damage" (Susan Chira, 1992). (The *Times* report is based on a report commissioned by the American Association of University Women Educational Foundation that in turn is based on work by hundreds of individual women and research groups.) What the report concludes for girls is also accurate for most women at most coeducational universities. Teachers pay less attention to girls than to boys. Boys talk more than girls in classrooms. Reports indicate that sexual harassment by peers is increasing. Textbooks still ignore or stereotype women. Girls learn almost nothing in their formal instruction about many issues critical for their lives, such as sexual harassment, violence against women, discrimination, and depression. At the moment, there is nothing to suggest that the new information technologies on campuses, from which so much is expected, will change this situation.

Lee Sproull and Sara Kiesler (1991) and others suggest that people who are peripheral in large organizations (e.g., because of low rank in the hierarchy) do relatively well on the nets. Indicators of race, age, physical abilities, and physical appearance disappear in "real-time chats" or in messages sent to be stored for later reading. Divisions, Sproull and Kiesler write, disappear. Except one. The signatures on most networks indicate the sex of the writer. As Angela Gunn (1991) argues in her article "Computer Bulletin Boards: Not Just Boy Toy," women are still The Other on most of the computer network systems in the world.

New Technology as Old Social Process

We do not question whether computer discussions could have a liberating influence within the university structure. These are frameworks for communicating that could offer new, inviting changes in the presently very gendered structure of academe. Computer conferences "exist on the intellectual margins of most traditional academic discourse communities in a new medium that is as wild and unsettled as any frontier" (Marilyn Cooper and Cynthia L. Selfe, 1990). However, if it is treated as a "frontier," to be conquered, subdued, and brought into line, we can be very sure that what we will soon have is more of the same practices that are repressive for women.

Despite all the potential the nets have for equalizing the influence of participants, we have evidence that women are experiencing on the nets much of the same kinds of trouble they experience in other conversations (see Barrie Thorne, Cheris Kramarae, and Nancy Henley [1983]; Karen Foss and Sonja Foss [1991]; Casey Miller and Kate Swift [1989]). If university administrators are really interested in providing a welcoming, comfortable climate for women in the office, classroom, and research lab, they can usefully turn attention now to the nets, as these are increasingly the places where education of many kinds happens. In fact, the problems that women experience in other conversations may be intensified on the nets. Beth Kevies, a user-services consultant at the Massachusetts Institute of Technology, says that "[p]eople do things on computers that they wouldn't dream of doing on any other medium." Obscenities, racial slurs, and vicious personal attacks are recorded from people who might not say such things in face-to-face interaction (quoted in David Wilson, 1991).[6]

Of course, not all conversations on electronic networks are the same.[7] Most public conversations take place on network bulletin boards such as Usenet, the Unix-based bulletin board network that can be accessed by any system connected to the Internet with the proper operating system. (In the U.S. there are an estimated 60,000 public access bulletin boards and an esti-

6) We have many examples from networks of women's concern with this problem. On a sociology network we found discussion of whether those who use concealing nicknames rather than their real names in making comments about affirmative action should even be replied to, and whether those who "flame" (send hot-tempered messages) should be "flamed back." The members of Systers, a network for women in computer science, are often harassed on other nets, and exchange information on how to deal with it (e.g. sending a copy of the offending message, along with a complaint, to the "postmaster" at the node from which the message originated.)

7) We thank WITS member Jenny Barrett for her contribution to this part of the discussion.

mated 10 million people who are regular callers to these public access bulletin board services.) Less public are the mailing lists, which are postings sent via the network to a specific list of people. The most private electronic conversations take place through private electronic mail (although, as with telephone conversations, electronic conversations can be "listened in on"). We suspect that the kind and extent of problems experienced by women and other "minorities" on these networks will vary depending on how public the forum and how cohesive the community of users. Bulletin boards as open networks have the most potential for abusive behavior. Lists are likely to retain more sense of community and sense of purpose, but exclusion from the conversation is more likely to have career repercussions for marginal groups. Private e-mail is similar to communication by telephone or letter, but the absence of aural cues and the speed of transmission may cause problems for communication.

Some Specific Problems

1. In almost any open network, men monopolize the talk.[8] The reasons are probably several. Young men may have more time to spend in front of their computers. Men, in general, are accustomed to talking more than women do in public conversations of various sorts (see annotated bibliography in Barrie Thorne, Cheris Kramarae, and Nancy Henley [1983]). If the topics women raise are seldom taken up by men on the networks, women may become less interested in network talk or feel that their issues are not very important. As Cynthia Selfe (1992) reports, students who are already assertive about their verbal group input, often because they enjoy a confidence born of privilege, feel freer to take more verbal space. WITS participant Ramona Curry notes that network members who want to take more time to think about responses or don't want to take up too much of others' time may find that discussions sweep by them.

Even open networks where the topic is women's issues are, we have found, over-run by men. For example, on this campus, we've checked the network called soc.women and have noticed that on some days only men have posted messages. On a national soc.women board, dominated by comments from men, one woman noted that even the women-only boards are not respected by men who cross-post to the women from other boards.[9]

The moderators of the newsgroup soc.feminism have noted that the men and women posting often have protracted disagreements on gender-neutral language, on the actual statistics on spouse-beating in comparing which sex is "worse off," and in the propriety of "women-only" events. These arguments have led many women to complain that soc.feminism is "too hostile" for them.

Women's topics and concerns are often not considered or taken seriously. Further, the "conversations" that take place may assume a degree of homogeneity that does not reflect the reality of the particular network.[10]

These should be concerns of anyone interested in collaboration and democracy. However, working toward gender equality in conversation, or in any setting, has not yet been made an important goal in most institutions.

8) When a draft of this paper was circulated among participants in the Lewis and Clark College Electronic Salon in April 1992, this point elicited numerous comments. Everyone seemed to have a study that verified our observations. For example, Jane Fraser made the following comments: "Here at Ohio State, we recently started osu.women. The consensus is that it is working fine, but only as a place for notices of meetings, etc. It is not a place where women can talk because–you guessed it–the men dominate and tend to pick apart word-by-word any woman's posting. We have recently started a private mailing list for women faculty and grad students in engineering–requests to be added will be verified." "Blade X," a male participant in the Electronic Salon, commented, "Cyberspace is elitist; cyberspace is exclusionary. For all the rhetoric and propaganda of eliminating barriers to participation it still remains the eminent domain of white, middle-class males."

9) From a 1988 soc.women network discussion:
Robert N: Lately in my reading of soc.men and soc.women, I've been noticing two phenomena:
–Articles (like this one, in fact : -) [smiley face] are heavily crossposted between soc.men and soc.women. In a recent batch, all but 5 of 40 articles in soc.men were crossposted to soc.women.
–Various soc.women readers complain that men are trying to dominate soc.women, when the group should be a forum for women's perspectives. Other readers think that the group should be a discussion of gender issues from anybody's point of view, and complain that they are being shoved out. (These men's articles are often among the articles crossposted to both groups.)
It might be a good idea, then, to create another...news-

group... so that soc.women and soc.men could go more towards being more a forum for the personal perspectives of women or men....
Mary: Go right ahead, Robert.... But you know what? I was here, on the net, the last time this was tried. We had a net.women, and a net.women-only.Guess what? Articles were cross-posted to net.women-only from net.women by men. Net.women-only was NOT respected by men....

10) Deborah Heath, organizer of the April 1992 Lewis and Clark College Electronic Salon, remarked, "In the absence of more complete cues about who is in our audience, some of us will assume that all share the same worldview... and... those who occupy privileged or "unmarked" social positions [male or white or straight or English-speaking, etc.] may be even more inclined to presume that their perspective is natural and universal."

11) In 1990 Peg Jennings wrote an open letter on a scientific network "...to those of you who assume that men are [scientists] and women are whores" after a series of limericks was posted. The discussion that followed was sometimes acrimonious. Some people sending messages said that the author of a particularly offending limerick was a staunch supporter of women in science and that it was a shame that he was being criticized in this way. Some women sent e-mail messages to individuals in the discussion, relating their own experiences of sexism in academe. After dozens of messages on this topic, the moderator decided that the issue of the limericks did not belong on the bulletin board: "[This] mailing list is a private mailing list for the discussion of *'technical'* issues only." He included the following directive: "Persons

2. Sexual harassment on the networks is a problem being reported by many women at many sites. The forms of sexual harassment vary. In some cases, women on the networks experience the types of sexist jokes and limericks that were once a part of many classroom lectures but now are increasingly discouraged by university administrators.[11] In other cases, women's complaints about the harassment they experience lead to hostile comments about the women.[12] Women who want to be respected scholars (which means avoiding being known as a trouble-maker, or as someone who questions the actions of respected men in the field) will be very hesitant about publicly pointing to sexist behavior. This silencing has serious consequences for interaction on individual nets, for disciplines and for the academy in general.

3. The climate of the nets may exclude many women and minorities from participating fully in the conversation. Men tend to use more assertive behavior than women. In addition to sending more messages, and introducing more new topics than do women, men tend to disagree more frequently with others. (See Cynthia L. Selfe and Paul R. Meyer [1990] for one valuable study; more research is needed on this.) "Flaming" (sending hot-tempered messages) is a issue that has received some attention by people on the networks. Yet seldom discussed is sex-related behavior on the networks and the impact of this kind of dominant behavior on women's participation.

4. We can expect an increase in high-tech titillation. *Penthouse,* with a circulation of 1.5 million, is one of the first mass media publications to become available electronically (Deirdre Carmody, 1991).The widespread interest in mass media pornography has always had implications for universities. For example, female students at universities across the country are increasingly daring to complain about *Playboy*-type posters in professors' offices and research labs, concerned about what the posters convey about the professors' attitudes toward women. Only recently have university administrators at many universities shown concern about these practices (and then usually only after women complain, often after they have changed courses or majors). Female scholars on campuses are also concerned about related electronic practices. University nets have been used to transmit pornography. At times this has been blatant, as when Usenet at the University of Washington carried electronically transferred digitized pornographic pictures (Elaine Richardson, 1991). In this case, the "sexually explicit drawings and photographs" were distributed to selected faculty members and students by the director of the university's Microcomputer Evaluation Center (*Chronicle of Higher Education*, Nov 13, 1991, pA22). At the University of Oregon the photographs were available on high-resolution display machines in the student computer labs.[12] Women at many other universities are reporting similar situations. Many of us have received unrequested body-parts "visuals" (e.g., "breasts" composed of computer keyboard letters and punctuation marks).

who continue this limerick thread will be removed from the list."
The woman who first complained about sexist limericks watched her computer screen as many of the network users commented on her action. A few examples: "If we let [her] get away with this raving attack on an innocent bit of humor, the next thing will be women trying to rewrite the English language, and then rewrite history, abolish men's and women's bathrooms..." "Get a grip... and stop treating men as all alike (simply because you are too blinded by your anger to think)." "By being a reactionary to limericks, you give a bad message about women. And that is exactly a cause that I fight. Your open letter is a condescending knee-jerk reaction." "[You contributed] to the stereotype of advocates of nonsexist writing as being brainless flakes."

12)After women students and faculty brought complaints, a notice was finally posted in the computer laboratory of the Computer and Information Science Department at the University of Oregon that states, in part, as follows: "The CIS Department has received reports of incidents of offensive and unprofessional behavior [in the lab]. Much of this behavior can be described as sexual harassment. At the very least, a small group of students has made it a very uncomfortable working environment and effectively driven away a large number of other students from the only place they can work on their class projects. Not surprisingly, this behavior also violates the University's Student Conduct Code.... The department views these reports very seriously, and is in the process of investigating them, as well as preparing an explicit statement of department policy regarding behavior in the workplace. In the meanwhile, reports of offensive

Implications for University Policy

Universities have the unique opportunity at this moment to change the structure of interaction on campuses. Without new policies guiding the use of these public nets, we will be losing a chance to plan new structures to benefit everyone in the university. Policies will need to deal not only with freedom of speech but also the protection of women and "minorities" on campus. (At times in the U.S. the First Amendment is discussed as if it is the Only Law of the Land. The laws provide for a variety of protections.) Computer networks provide a forum for many kinds of debates. University policy could encourage open debate for everyone, including women, but this would entail revisions in policies and behavior. A few suggestions to begin discussions:

1. Women-only forums for speech. The literature is clear: men are more interested in having mixed-sex conversations than women are. Women are more likely to give men plenty of time, space, and consideration than vice versa. Separatism is not necessarily what women want for their discussions, but until gender equality becomes a reality in a wide variety of settings, women need both access to the public nets and some safe forums for their conversations. (In case some readers believe that only "those radical feminists" want women-only forums, they should know that there are all kinds of women-only nets, including a fundamentalist-Christian board [Angela Gunn, 1991].) On women-only nets, the talk is more candid and the topics, unlike those on "regular" boards, are controlled by women.[13] Because impostors are present, perhaps prevalent, on the nets, university policies should deal with those who gain trust and confidences by presenting themselves as other than they are, sometimes with devastating results to those who trusted (Lindsy Van Gelder, 1985).

2. Training, including instruction in the issues above, for the moderators, who decide what is allowed on the nets and who have the right to censor material they do not think belongs there. The moderators would learn about the issues introduced above and about ways of dealing with people who express disrespect for others on the nets.

3. Warnings for new participants and reminders for long-time participants. We could make a part of the responsibilities of organizers and "owners" of networks the warning to users that the networks are not totally private or safe. Deborah Heath, in the Electronic Salon, pointed out that "[t]he informal mode of most communiqués, the rapidity of response, and the fact that many of us can send and receive messages within the familiar surroundings of home all work to create, it seems to me, a sense of intimacy or connectedness with others in a discussion group. But... this "safe" intimacy is partial and to some extent illusory." Unknown others, with more interest in playing games with the systems than in ensuring confidentiality of discussions can, for example, "listen in" and send "fake messages" with false names and addresses.

4. A grievance procedure for complaints of sexual harassment on the nets.

behavior should be directed to [several names] or to any CIS faculty member. Please remember that the appearance and atmosphere of the University facilities (that includes computing labs) should be conducive to their educational goals. Professional courtesy and respect are not only the norm but the rule to be enforced." (We thank Sarah Douglas, CIS Department, University of Oregon, for this material, and for her comments on an earlier version of this paper.)

13) One man who spends a great deal of time on the nets said, in response to discussions of women-only nets, something like this: I spend about four hours a day on the net, talking to my girlfriend, and on the scuba diving bulletin board, etc. It's all there for me. Then I hear you talking about these other nets that I can't access–your Handsnet, and dog and cat net or whatever. And I find it really *frightening* that you are out there communicating with each other, and I can't get to it." For many women, of course, access to nets–and time to use them–is very limited.

14) During the Electronic Salon, "Blade X" (a man) commented, "I have yet to see a post by a migrant farm worker or a homeless person. Both groups who are fairly immune to the viruses of feminism and/or communication technology. When dealing with technology, always ask who is invited? and who is excluded?"

This should be part of the sexual harassment policy of any institution that sponsors (or allows) electronic network communication. Users should be told that sexual harassment will not be tolerated, the prohibited behaviors should be defined, and punishments should be spelled out. Users should be given details on how, when, and where they can complain about harassment. The policy should also take a strong, explicitly detailed stand against retaliation; otherwise many people experiencing harassment will fear reporting it. (See William Petrocelli and Barbara Kate Repa [1992] for excellent information on how effective policies can be written and enforced.)

5. Periodic reports, to a central body, on the number and types of complaints and action taken. These reports could also include assessment of the conversations on the nets – number and length of postings and control of topics by women and men. They could also include a yearly profile of the subscribers and the participants, so network users could find out who was participating and who was silently listening in. The reports and assessments would differ depending upon the makeup and issues of the network. Some models are available. For example, one national network community (discussing aspects of the research field of computers and writing) decided to try a period of 20 days during which participants used real names and 20 days during which participants could use their real name or a pseudonym. The researchers (Cynthia L. Selfe and Paul R. Meyer, 1991) who decided to analyze the interaction during those days found that messages were sent by 18 men and 15 women from 16 states. Men contributed twice as many messages and 40% more words; high-profile (determined in part by publications) members contributed more than twice the number of messages and words than did low-profile members. Participation by both women and men increased during the pseudonym-optional period. While the option of using pseudonyms seemed to have a particular appeal for women, it did not result in any restructuring of conference power relationships. Perhaps of most importance, the experiment prompted more explicit attention and discussion of power issues.

6. Clarification of what will be considered offensive messages. (Who will decide whether something is repugnant and objectionable?) Universities concerned about the prevailing chilly climates for women on campus could organize guidelines for behavior that show particular concern with the problems which women and "minorities" often experience in conversations with others. The guidelines offered by Howard Rosenbaum and Gregory Newby (1990) might be used as an aid in establishing the agreed-upon etiquette of network communications. Other useful examples are available from some of the nets, such as DOROTHYL, a network discussion group, organized by a group of women librarians, for lovers of the mystery genre. (They considered limiting DOROTHYL [named after Dorothy L. Sayers, the writer of mysteries] to women participants, but realized that it was likely that "men would sneak on with anonymous [identifications] to join in DOROTHYL's energizing discussions.") Among the directions they include is "Be tolerant of newcomers.

Do not abuse new users of computer networks for their ignorance – be patient...."

7. Explicit explanations about determining who can create a network bulletin board on what topics.[14] The person in charge of approving and setting up new bulletin boards and newsgroups generally uses his [sic] own judgment. One such person on a university campus states: "I have to make continuing choices based on what provides the best value to the University community.... My general theory is that if a group has some value to myself or [the computer center], I'll create it soon after the newsgroup is posted once it shows signs of life."

8. Explicit discussion of the differing access to networks, both inside and outside academe. Men are overwhelmingly the primary users of the nets. Many male students expect to use them in jobs outside the academy, and ask about access in job interviews. What are the implications of this differential use for women's jobs of the future? We know that women, in very low-paying and physically debilitating jobs, are making the computer chips that middle-class men are using for recreation, communication, and job fulfillment. What is happening with the sex hierarchies in academe is not divorced from the sex hierarchies worldwide. The increasing number of city Freenets (free to users, supported by community individuals, groups, or businesses) does not solve all access problems. Some people can afford modems for home use; others can't afford the bus fare to get to the modems in the libraries or other public places. Also, women, especially older women, often trained to think that they will break machinery if they try to use it, may not feel as comfortable using the networks unless special efforts are made to involve them in the Freenet programs.

Getting even these initial relatively minor responses from the academy would not be a simple matter. As women's studies research has made very clear, universities (and most other institutions) have taught sex discrimination, if not explicitly at least very well. The rhetoric about the importance of diversity and equality in universities has been in place for some time, but equity in practice has been very slow in following. Now, with the so-called electronic-information revolution in the "West," we have a wonderful opportunity for some administrators, staff, faculty, and students to take specific actions that could have an edifying influence on every member of academia–and many others.

Acknowledgments

We worked with Maureen Ebben during the first year of the WITS colloquium. We appreciate the discussions with her that contributed to this paper. We also appreciate the comments of WITS member Jenny Barrett, Sarah Douglas at the University of Oregon, and of the participants in the Electronic Salon of the Gender Symposium at Lewis and Clark College, April 1992.

References

Adler, Richard (1988). *Seniornet: Toward a National Community of Computer-Using Seniors. Forum Report #5, Aspen Institute Project on Enhancing the Social Benefits of New Electronic Technologies.* New York, N.Y., Aspen Institute.

Brown, Evan (1991). "On Line in the Big Sky." *Missoula Independent,* November 14, 10.

Carmody, Deirdre (1990). "New President at *Penthouse* Looks Beyond Printed Page." *The New York Times,* December 1, C1, C8.

Chira, Susan (1992). "Bias Against Girls Is Found Rife in Schools, With Lasting Damage." *The New York Times*, February 12, A1, A10.

Cooper, Marilyn M. and Cynthia L. Selfe (1990). "Computer Conferences and Learning: Authority, Resistance, and Internally Persuasive Discourse." *College English*, 52:8, 847-869.

Foss, Karen and Sonja Foss (1991). *Women Speak: The Eloquence of Women's Lives*. Prospect Heights, Ill.: Waveland Press.

Gunn, Angela (1991). "Computer Bulletin Boards Not Just Boy Toy." *New Directions for Women*, November-December, 7.

Hall, Roberta M. and Bernice Sandler (1982). "The Classroom Climate: A Chilly One for Women." *Project on the Status and Education of Women.* Washington, D.C.: Association of American Colleges.

Kramarae, Cheris (1989). "Computers, Communication and Education: Science Fiction and Fantasies." Conference on Rhetoric and Technology, Houghton, Mich., Michigan Technological University, October.

Miller, Casey and Kate Swift (1989). *Words and Women: New Language in New Times*, 2nd ed. Garden City, N.Y.: Doubleday.

Petrocelli, William and Barbara Kate Repa (1992). *Sexual Harassment on the Job*. Berkeley: Nolo Press.

Richardson, Elaine (1991). "U. Washington deletes erotica from computer network." *The Daily Illini*, October 31, 4.

Rosenbaum, Howard and Gregory B. Newby (1990). "An Emerging Form of Human Communication: Computer Networking." *ASIS '90: Proceedings of the 53rd ASIS Annual Meeting*, v. 27. November 4-8, Toronto, Ontario.

Selfe, Cynthia L. (1992). "Computer-based Conversations and the Changing Nature of Collaboration." In Janis Forman (Ed.), *New Visions of Collaborative Writing*. Portsmouth, N.H.: Boynton/Cook, 147-169.

Selfe, Cynthia and Paul R. Meyer (1991). "Testing Claims for On-line Conferences." *Written Communication,* 8:2, 162-192.

Smith, Judy and Ellen Balka (1988). "Chatting on a Feminist Computer Network." In Cheris Kramarae (Ed.), *Technology and Women's Voices*. New York: Routledge & Kegan Paul/Methuen, 82-97.

Sproull, Lee and Sara Kiesler (1991). *Connections: New Ways of Working in the Networked Organization*. Cambridge, Mass.: Massachusetts Institute of Technology Press.

Thorne, Barrie, Cheris Kramarae, and Nancy Henley (Eds.) (1983). *Language, Gender and Society*. Rowley, Mass.: Newbury House.

Van Gelder, Lindsy (1985). "The Strange Case of the Electronic Lover." *Ms*. October, 94-104, 117, 123, 124.

Wilson, David L. (1991). "Computer-related Ethical Problems are Focus of Conference on Values." *The Chronicle of Higher Education,* September 4, A31.

WITS Colloquium Digests

The heading "Women, Information Technology, and Scholarship" encompasses many themes and concerns. During the 1991-1992 academic year the participants and speakers of the WITS colloquium discussed several issues and took part in workshops in labs throughout the UIUC campus. In this section we give short digests of the talks by several of the speakers. These digests do not provide the full arguments developed by the speakers, but they do give an idea of some of the key themes raised during the WITS sessions.

Changes in Academic Concepts of Privacy, Originality, and Ownership of Ideas

Dale Spender

16 October 1991

Although women have been quite successful in publishing, women have not been in positions of influence. They could not decide what was published, or get women's books on the shelves, until they set up their own presses.

It is not enough to have, as Virginia Woolf put it, 500 pounds a year and a room of one's own; you also need a press. I think you have to control the means of production. Feminist presses created the market for women's books that now the mainstream can service more efficiently, and with greater resources, than can the feminist presses. During the past year, several feminist presses have gone out of existence.The women's presses are in great trouble, teetering on the edge, as are many publishers at the moment because there is actually a huge shrinkage in publishing.

The knowledge that women have encoded in women's books is very definitely at risk at the moment. One of the reasons women became proficient in publishing, the reason they had success in publishing, is that it wasn't the primary medium of information anymore. It wasn't contested in the same way it used to be. There was some room for women to get in and set up publishing companies. As men have moved to electronic media, there has been some space for women to develop women's presses. But, in fact, I think women's knowledge, which is encoded almost exclusively in those books, is more at risk now than at any other period in our history–because of the transfer from one medium to the next.

I know of no women's software company, hardware company, or analysis company. I'm sure there are women in all aspects of the electronic media, but there's nobody that I can talk to about these issues. I can't go to a women's television station and say why don't you make these programs; I can't go to women's newspapers and say what's the alternative to the way the Hill-Thomas hearings have been analyzed. I don't know of an all-day women's radio station that could provide an alternative to the news.... It's very, very difficult at the moment when it comes to this new medium, when we're in an electronic mode. I know of a few women who can explain things to me, but where are the women who can make the decisions?

I don't think we even begin to understand the implications of what's happening (in the shift to the electronic era) when we are so excluded. What I see at the moment is the same for all systems of government in our history – men are doing the producing and women are going to be in the position of consuming.

The historical development of print actually made generations – millions of people – readers who previously would not have been readers. Of course, what the electronic media are going to do is make millions of people writers who wouldn't previously have been writers. Are we going to call it democratization of information, or the deprofessionalization of the writer?

I keep saying these days that indexers are the most important people in the world, that what's being set up in the new electronic media is almost a schema for how we're going to organize the information. It's going to be absolutely vital and there's very little discussion about it in widespread circles. Indexing is absolutely fundamental. I've pointed out what would happen if I wrote an article on witches, about these wonderful, marvelous, magnificent women who lived in the Middle Ages and who got burnt by all those wicked men. If I handed it over to a software programmer who indexed it under "evil women" and "satanic practices," I'd never find it again.

The concept of copyright only applies to a fixed text. It is just absolutely absurd when you start applying it to an electronic medium.

The whole idea of privacy is being changed by the electronic media. It's not just about the government having a database on where we live or what our credit ratings are, it's much more fundamental. Think about the ways in which your luggage is searched in airports – that would be inconceivable fifty years ago in terms of invasion of privacy. Now, there are video cameras on all over the place.

Publishing in an Electronic Environment

Phyllis Hall

13 November 1991

What really excites me about being in my position is that we are moving into an electronic environment, although the meaning of that is not the same for everyone. Is it desktop publishing? Is it the on-line catalogue? Or is it that conversation you have on e-mail? Video conferencing? CD-ROM? I am especially concerned here about the entire process of publishing, especially scholarly publishing as a totally electronic process. We are a long way from that end result.

At the moment there are issues upon issues upon issues, with few clear answers. Here, I give a view from outside the university.

Publishing in that "simple" time after World War II, when we knew how things should be, we had constructs that we thought worked – like the nuclear family. And, of course, printed journals. Scholars who received grants to do research were expected to publish, and that required a publisher. So there were publishers who supported the whole system of peer review, and the publishers' responsibilities went beyond that. They had to take the quality-controlled, validated research and present it in that wonderful form we know as the printed journal. They followed an enormous number of conventions so that the journal would have the "right" style of referencing and the "right" kind of format. Why not one reference style to make life easier? Rather, every academic society had to have its commas in the right place to distinguish it from other societies. People argued with passion over colons. Beyond following the proper conventions, the publisher was responsible for letting others know that this material was available and ensuring its wide distribution. Publishers worked hand in glove with libraries. After World War II, academic libraries were relatively affluent. They could buy in quantity. They had a distinct mission – to collect, collect, collect. Large collections were a mark of a great university. This construct of scholar to publisher to library to scholar worked well for a number of decades.

In the late 1960s and 1970s, new players began to appear. Some people started to do abstracting to make finding information easier. They became the first electronic publishers. They also generated a great deal of conflict because primary publishers viewed them as parasites. It took many years for primary publishers to accept that the secondary publisher helped the primary, and to relax those animosities. Subscription agents were more easily recognized as necessary service providers, gathering all of a library's orders and dealing directly with publishers.

The late 1970s and early 1980s saw early computer systems, and with them the reopening of the dialogue on the "paperless" society. However, publishers responded by saying, "Remember microfilm (and remember the suckers who invested)." Some turf battles developed on major campuses between librarian information specialists using (unfriendly) electronic databases, and strange academic computing types who began to infringe on the budgets of librarians. When the pain of tight budgets became intolerable, and the need for more computer support a top priority, librarians' attention was directed toward the publishers of expensive academic journals as the cause of all problems.

Libraries responded by changing their mission of collect, collect, collect to focus on more efficient access. Librarians still believed in collecting and archiving, of course, but now there was more discussion about dividing what each library collected and about more cooperation among libraries.

With the increased use of networks, such as Internet, some scholars and librarians are saying that perhaps we don't need publishers at all. The abstracting services are trying to become more user-friendly so no intermediary librarian is needed. Subscription agencies are developing current awareness service and document delivery capabilities. Libraries and abstracting services can send information directly to the people who want it in the form they need it, printed or electronic, and often with more speed than publishers. For a while, many of these nonpublishers have talked as if electronic publishing did not cost anyone anything.

Meanwhile, publishers continue to be concerned about the work in the editorial offices, about bringing quality control to publishing, and about telling the world what publications are available. And some publishers are wondering, "Why am I investing all this money and then seeing the material being given away or sold by others? Why don't *we* send it out to users, because it doesn't need to go to a library electronically when I can send it to the user in Cincinnati or Sioux Falls. And perhaps we should be only printing books on demand. The technology is here."

Like a game of musical chairs, it seems as if there might not be room for all of the original participants. With so many difficult questions to be answered, the dialogue between scholar, library, and publisher must not be allowed to break down.

There are many very positive changes, one being the Internet with thousands of networks and no centralized control. We can see that it could be the most democratizing, least hierarchical environment we've had, fostering collaboration, teamwork, and give and take. These sound like feminist values. But women have taken an arm's-length approach to much of the new technology. Hierarchies may become built in. This is a time for women to become very active, before controllers take control – a chaotic time, but an exciting one.

Imagining the Ideal Information Technology

Marie T. Banich
Betsy Wilson

22 January 1992

During this two-hour workshop, WITS members collaborated in six groups of four to design the ideal information technology. By employing cooperative learning techniques borrowed from the classroom, the workshop leaders engaged the participants in an inclusive design process.

The leaders used issue-based minilectures and anecdotes to frame the four questions used to focus the design process:

1. What are the physical characteristics of the ideal information technology?
2. What information should the ideal information technology provide?
3. How do you want to learn to use this ideal information technology?
4. What are the issues of control and privacy associated with the ideal information technology?

After each small group addressed each question, the leaders recorded the ideas flowing from the lively, collaborative dialogues using flipcharts. By the end of the workshop, a colorful, creative, and innovative ideal information technology had emerged.

Summary Statement

The ideal information technology is mobile (remote controllable, solar-powered, usable around the world, available as a lapel button), compact, flexible in size, personally customized, sensitive to users and to the environment, accommodating of multiple input and output modes, and inexpensive.

The ideal information technology provides conceptual quilt-piecing, nonlinear information coding, expert problem-solving systems, translations of jargon into understandable language, a broad array of information (including telephone numbers and household information), and retrieval customized to one's personal history.

Learning and training would be done through "mentor mom," "computer goddess," or "parole officer" models. WITS members want monitoring of progress with feedback as we work (both within and between sessions, through a toll-free e-mail number, and with split screens), compassionate and sympathetic peers and teachers, active participation in the learning process, and multiple learning modes.

Talking on InterChange

Gail Hawisher

5 February 1992

In early fall 1991, fifteen WITS members met in the Department of English's Professional Writing Classroom with its networked MacIntosh computers. Our purpose was to try out InterChange and discuss the possibility of a national Center for Women and Information Technology. InterChange, a product of the Daedalus Group of Austin, Texas, is a synchronous communication program that allows all participants to talk together at once, without waiting for one another to take turns. The program divides the screen into two parts, with each participant writing a comment in the lower portion of the screen and then clicking on a button to send the message to the upper part of the screen where everyone can read it. Participants compose and send messages while reading their colleagues' messages as they appear and scroll by on the upper portion of the screen.

Although the program is sometimes disorienting (many messages scroll rapidly by at once), it encourages everyone to contribute to the discussion rather than just a few, and provides participants with a written transcript of the discussion. For the hour and a half session, Gail Hawisher posed the following written prompt to WITS members to start off the discussion: If we were to create a Center for Women and Information Technology, what purposes would it serve and how would we organize it?

As with all our discussions, electronic and otherwise, many great ideas emerged. Jeanie Taylor wanted us to be sure to think about outreach programs that would "give women opportunities to join the computer age," and Jo Kibbee argued for more "hands-on workshops" for women to learn the new technologies. Jenny Barrett wants more research – both on and by women – to explore issues related to why women of various ages, races, and backgrounds eschew technology in ways that their brothers don't. Leigh Estabrook suggested an electronic bulletin board where women could use one another as resources for their research; Linda Smith said that such a center needed to be "a focal point for research, instructional support, and outreach combined"; and Cheris Kramarae argued that it must deal with technology assessment and be a place "where women can work through the issues and projects" related to policy-making and computers. Ramona Curry concurred, saying that a such a center must work "to influence policy on the development and dissemination of technologies." Apple's Laura Ege volunteered the idea of women speakers for a lecture series, and Sarah Wasserman suggested that the Fund for the Improvement of Postsecondary Education might be a good place to look for funding.

All these ideas flew over the network, sparking new exchanges, new plans, new perspectives – and sometimes new discomfort. While all agreed that Inter-Change was an exciting technology, some thought it was too fast and favored the quick response rather than the thoughtful response. So many ideas came and went that we feared we couldn't give them the attention they deserved. By encouraging multiple, synchronous conversations, InterChange provided something that was neither talk nor writing. In short, while the many excellent exchanges over the network were invigorating, we often needed to work very hard to keep our WITS about us.

Linking Women: Computer Networks as a Feminist Resource

Judy Smith

18 March 1992

We began our Montana project with the realization that we need to be involved in addressing the strategies that promote economic development. Because we're feminists and concerned about women, we wanted to talk about strategies that promote opportunities for women and their economic development; so we started WORD (Women's Opportunity and Resource Development, Inc.) and developed projects specifically geared toward women and low-income people.

Although we are based in Missoula, we serve women throughout Montana. By means of computer networks, we link up with the other women's programs in the state. For example, we have thirteen displaced homemaker programs, and we have several welfare and WORD training programs all connected by electronic networks.

Through WORD we provide loans that enable women to start their own businesses and become self-sufficient. Women begin with skills they already possess, and develop a local to regional market. We give them the tools and capital to move into these markets and earn some income.

In 1986 the Big Sky Telegraph was set up with the idea that rural schools and three hundred communities in Montana should be linked to each other. One of the important concepts of this network is that not only are the hardware and software provided, but a person, a community telegrapher, is also there to assist people in getting on the system.

What are some of the barriers to women's use of technology? One may be socialization. We're not raised to see women as the ones who use technology in our culture. Girls are not praised and rewarded for using technology in the same ways boys are. Another barrier is the lack of rewards for women. Using computers has to be worth your time, you have to see the result. It's not enough to say "this is good for you, do it" – which is how we tend to approach computer use. Women are often reluctant users of computers, so there need to be appropriate rewards to move them through the barriers of computer use. In working with trying to get women on computer conferences we've been struggling with how to have the rewards clear and short-term.

A related issue is how we train people to get on computer networks. I think we do a poor job. The training is not based on learning theory. Rather, it is based on the fact that most of the people who developed networks are computer hackers, men, who take their own way of doing things and believe that it is a viable training method. Most people have very frustrating experiences with learning how to participate in computer networks. They may manage to get on the network, but it is usually in spite of their training, not because of it.

To address the problems in computer training for women, we have sought to identify the relevant rewards for women. We have taken the novel approach of asking women what they want to accomplish through using the technology and incorporating that as a reward.

We have thirteen women's centers linked around the state of Montana, plus some other women who are interested in the women's network. One project we have teaches women with small businesses how to do their cash flow accounts on the computer. Another project is the Montana Women's Lobby, a women's organization that lobbies for women's issues in the legislature. During the legislative session some changes in language come up, so one thing we do is get the lobbyist on-line and discuss the issues on the computer network. This project maximizes our sense of success. This network really works, it empowers us.

Agency in the Age of Information

H. Patricia Hynes

8 April 1992

Science journalism conveys little about the ethics and politics of science, the structure of scientific institutions, the priorities that guide technological decisions, and the ideologies of science in the making. The communication from both the pharmaceutical industry that developed the new chemical abortifacient RU 486 and its supporters, including women's health professionals and reproductive rights activists, has four common characteristics: playing down the risks and pain for women; branding it the technology of choice for women when it is, in reality, the doctors' technology of choice; fostering a supermarket mentality of "the more choices the better" with women as consumers of health care; and exaggerating the drug's value.

The Institute of Women and Technology, a nonprofit feminist think tank that I direct, released a critical report on RU 486, which is now being sold in France and England. (RU 486 is strongly endorsed by most U.S. reproductive rights groups and liberal politicians and banned by the Bush administration.) One section of our report examines the claims for the drug made by the developer and by the media. It has been called "private." In fact, it is given under strict medical supervision in specialized centers that are no more private than abortion centers. RU 486 will "give more women control over their fertility," claimed the developer, Etienne Baulieu. In fact, it is less successful and carries more risks than conventional suction abortion, and has many contraindications making it unsafe and unusable for many women. It has been offered hyperbolically as the solution to the 200,000 deaths of women worldwide due to botched abortions. In fact, these women are dying in countries where abortion is illegal and primary health care is unavailable. RU 486 is now administered with prostaglandins, which require refrigeration, and the entire procedure requires medical backup not available in the "Third World," nor to poor women in the U.S., for that matter.

Science is deliberately split from public policy in agencies like the Environmental Protection Agency (EPA). The clean split between those who ask questions and those who decide answers in the EPA is a form of reification through role that makes people small and docile and can turn environmental research scientists into people who abdicate their own insights and do what they are told. Researchers do research but don't make value judgements on their findings. Managers think about the findings and make policy and decisions.

It is not so much the plodding method of science but the freedom from loyalties that fetter which is at stake here. Who sounds the warnings these days on the medicalization of women's bodies, the loss of biodiversity, the need to act sooner rather than later about global climate change? Independent, nonaligned scientists, environmentalists, and feminist health experts do so.

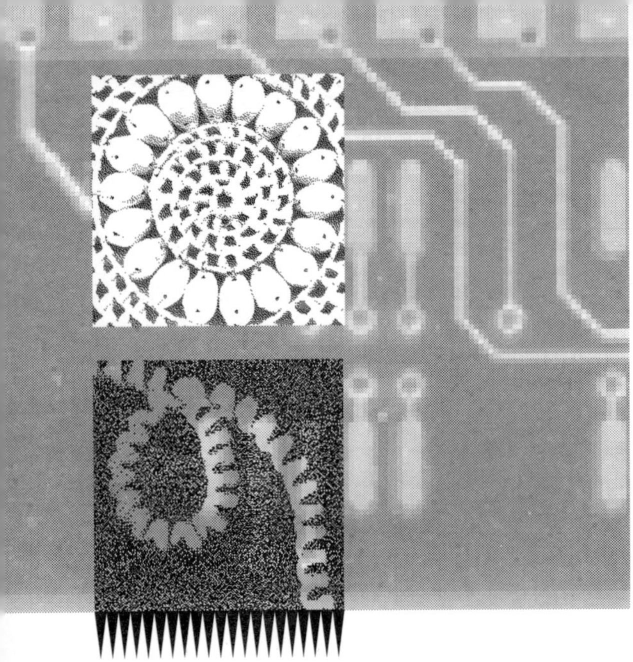

WITS and the Joint Academic Network (JANET)

Jo Kibbee

29 April 1992

(WITS member Jo Kibbee, Head of Central Reference Services in the UIUC Library, received funding in the spring of 1992 from the Campus Research Board and the Library Research and Publications Committee (UIUC) to conduct research on library applications of the U.K.'s Joint Academic Network (JANET). The idea for the project grew directly from Jo's participation in WITS during the fall and spring semesters. Below is her description of the role WITS played in the project.)

During the spring of 1992, I traveled to England to research the U.K.'s Joint Academic Network and its evolving role in British libraries. Linking universities and polytechnics, research centers, the British Library, and the national libraries of Scotland and Wales, JANET (like the Internet) holds the potential to revolutionize access to bibliographic, numeric, and text databases. I was particularly concerned with issues such as training and continuing education for accessing the network, the impact of electronic networking on reference and information services in libraries, and network policy. In practical terms, my work provided an excellent opportunity to utilize electronic technologies to communicate with colleagues overseas (using e-mail to set up meetings) while fostering a greater understanding of the complex issues involved in effectively utilizing a seemingly limitless resource–the electronic network.

Much of the credit for the development of this project goes to WITS. From its inception, WITS served as a forum for exploring new technologies in teaching, research, and scholarly communication, with a focus on advocating the meaningful participation of women as developers and beneficiaries of these technologies. Securing a viable role in this brave new world requires understanding the issues, acquiring specific technical skills, and receiving encouragement and support, and WITS is instrumental in generously providing these. Several WITS colloquia focused on the potential that data communications and electronic networking hold for expanding access to information. Members and guest speakers examined current and future capabilities of computer networks, with a focus on electronic mail, electronic publishing, and access to electronic databases. Discussions and explorations ranged from local to international networks, and touched directly on the library. To translate ideas into action, WITS also provides the opportunity to acquire skills necessary for navigating electronic environments, such as e-mail. Perhaps most importantly, however, through contact with women who have the desire and ability to become empowered by technology, WITS offers an enthusiastic and supportive environment in which intellectual (and technological) curiosity can prosper.

Kathleen, what typeface do you think we should use? I prefer a font that reflects a machine yet has personal characteristics.

The typewriter fits that description as a mid-mainstream technology that was and is significant to women on many levels. Prestige Elite is a font designed to reflect the appearance of typewriting but with uniformity of weight, size, and proportion.

C O N N E C T I O N S

women, information technology and scholarship

As a beta-site for Linotype-Hell, a type foundry, we were sent a new package of fonts titled *Type before Gutenberg* to experiment with. HERCULANUM is an upper case medieval style interpreted for computer use.

"Studies in cognitive psychology and anthropology demonstrate that the nature of the gathering of information has always been organizational, nothing more. . . . Freed from the tyranny of verbal literacy, the truly elegant and economical nature of human thought is now visible, and legibility, a dream of thought controlled by spatial order...".

— Frances Butler

Designing a Visual Identity: Empathic Response to Content

A process piece by
Kathleen Chmelewski
and Nan Goggin

As part of a design discipline associated with modernism, the "logo" traditionally has a fixed meaning and a rigid method of application as typified by standards manuals where logo variations are rigorously defined. For the WITS logo, we consciously decided to avoid the mythology of the singular. Instead, we embraced diversity as a far more dimensional solution; metaphorically represented by variations on a theme. As we developed the visual identity (*depicted at various stages on the right*) we asked the following questions. What icons and symbols might represent a holistic approach to information technologies? Would looking for parallels in the natural world provide us with a model for a more inclusive approach to technology? What historical models could we use to represent a system of support and sharing? How does one iconographically represent all the concepts listed below; or do we need to infer, suggest, or inspire the connections instead?

Nan, to establish a visual identity for WITS we need to distill a range of information; the WITS women are making connections between widely disparate systems of thought!

scholarship
computers
information
representation
holistic
interdisciplinary
history
independence
interdependence
networking
technology
nature

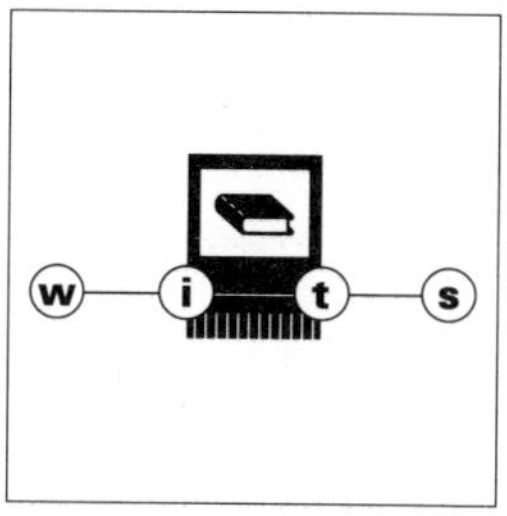

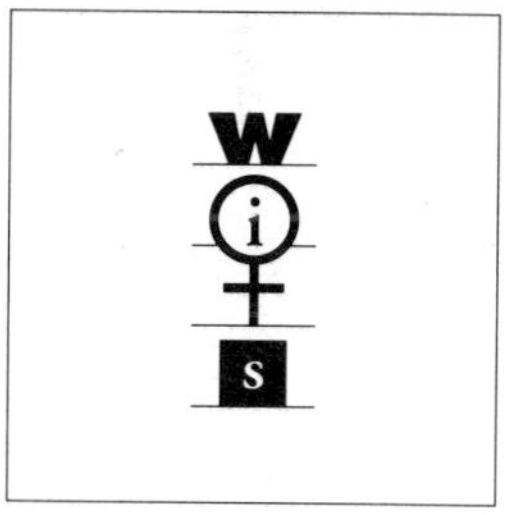

Women and Information Technology: An Annotated Bibliography

Maureen Ebben
Maria Mastronardi

The following is an annotated bibliography on the topic of women and information technology. In this introduction, we briefly discuss the process of compiling the bibliography and comment on why we chose to include these specific texts.

Going into the project, we considered the topic of women and information technology to be a broad one and felt confident that we would have little trouble locating appropriate sources. We envisioned building a compilation of feminist works on information technologies, with writings documenting women's experiences with all kinds of technology at every stage of development. Soon we realized that published texts that specifically address the nexus of women and information technology were few and far between, and those that were in existence were often not readily available.

Our project shifted. We decided to loosen our constraints, and cast our net widely in order to capture the mood and range of current discussions about information technology by not only feminists but also social theorists and critics more generally. Although we were primarily interested in texts written from a feminist perspective, we also considered texts that contained an awareness and sensitivity to the social and cultural components of information technologies. Aiming to be as inclusive as possible, we decided to include works on a whole range of diverse but relevant and related issues, including, for example, those that were related specifically to women, such as the impact of new technology on women's employment, "classic" works by feminists on the masculinist bias of technology, feminist assessments of technology, case studies of women's on-line databases and networks, handbooks aimed at fostering women's computer literacy, studies that document the gender gap in computer use, and conference proceedings in which issues of women and information technology are addressed.

We also felt it necessary to include discussions about issues of information technology more generally, including, for example, those that addressed literature from the sociology of knowledge to the social construction of science, the use and effectiveness of microcomputers in schools, critical treatises on the history of technology including the adverse impact of industrial technology and the myriad problems associated with the information society, discussions on artificial intelligence and the global assembly line in the electronics industry, issues of new information technologies in organizational and university contexts, and theorizations on the meaning and uses of hypermedia.

Although our net was cast widely, it was still necessary for us to place some restrictions on which texts would be included. For instance, because we were interested in critical texts, the immense body of writing on technical aspects of information technology was omitted, and because we were focusing our efforts on issues of women and information technology, the insightful literature on women and reproductive technology was omitted as well. Several of the sources included were identified through on-line databases with electronic searching techniques – interestingly, the subject and content of this bibliography (information technology) was employed in its creation. We experienced firsthand the joys and frustrations of using new information technologies and techniques for research and literature searches. In the annotations, we sought not only to give a brief synopsis of the main theme of the text but also to indicate our own sense of the volume's usefulness for someone interested in issues of gender and information technology. We note the shortcomings of works that omit considerations of gender and class. This is not to say that our annotations are scathing critiques of the texts; indeed, we have grown rather fond of the texts included in this bibliography. We feel that each work makes a valuable contribution to the women and information technology discussion.

It is crucial to mention that we do not presume this bibliography to be comprehensive or exhaustive. Rather, we see it as representative of the range of arguments and discussions currently circulating in published material on information technology. Like the texts currently in circulation, this bibliography is open to modification, change, and revision. We welcome suggestions for additional sources to augment and complement this ongoing work.

Finally, but most importantly, we want to acknowledge our indebtedness to a number of very supportive and helpful women. We want to thank Beth Stafford-Vaughan of the Women's Studies Library for bringing key authors and titles to our attention as well as for her help in tracking down hard-to-find sources. We want to thank H. Jeanie Taylor of the Center for Advanced Study for her insightful ideas and encouragement. We also want to thank the women of the Women, Information Technology, and Scholarship colloquium of the Center for Advanced Study at the UIUC for providing a stimulating context in which to explore these issues. Finally, we are especially fortunate to have Cheris Kramarae as our advisor; we are grateful for her characteristic patience, good humor, and intellectual incisiveness.

Abir-Am, Prira (Ed.) (1987). *Uneasy Careers and Intimate Lives: Women in Science, 1789-1979.* New Brunswick, N.J.: Rutgers University Press.
Collection of twelve essays by women historians of science covering general topics such as women's role in early 19th century French and North American science. Also included are biographies of scientists Maria Mitchell, Clemence Royer, Sofia Kovalevskaia, Marie Curie, Cecilia Payne-Gaposchkin, and Dorothy Wrinch.

Adas, Michael (1991). *Machines as the Measure of Men: Science, Technology and Ideologies of Western Dominance.* Ithaca, N.Y.: Cornell University Press.
An uncritical, masculinist account of the history of technology. Adas' thesis asserts that the mastery of nature lay at the heart of Europe's comparison of itself with other cultures, specifically Africa, China, and India.

Adiseshiah, M. (Ed.) (1985). *Science and Technology for Women.* Madras: Affiliated East-West Press Pvt. Ltd.
Collection of papers presented on March 25 and 26, 1985, at the Vivekananda Auditorium of Anna University for the Seminar on Science and Technology for Women, sponsored by the Tamil Nadu State Council for Science and Technology, in consultation with the Department of Science and Technology, Government of India. Topics addressed include employment patterns of women in research and development organizations, the status and responsibility of women in science and technology, women's roles in reserach, the impact of new technologies on women's employment and status, and experiences of rural women with technology transfer.

Ahmed, Iftikhar (Ed.) (1985). *Technology and Rural Women: Conceptual and Empirical Issues.* Boston: G. Allen and Unwin.
Claims to bring a rigorous analysis of implications for choice of techniques and allocation of resources said to be lacking in the literature on gender-based inequalitites in technological development. Shows how traditional macroeconomic theories are inadequate for the analysis of the impact of technological change on rural women, and how the prediction of such impact is made difficult by the intricacies in the labor process and the institutionalization of female labor in different ways in different countries and situations.

Albury, David (1985). "'E.T.': Technology and Masculinity." *Radical Science,* 16, 135-149.
The author sets forth an analysis of the film "E.T.," arguing that it allows us to understand masculinity and, inter alia, its linkages with technology and technological choice.

Alic, Margaret (1986). *Hypatia's Heritage: A History of Women in Science From Antiquity to the Late Nineteenth Century.* London: The Women's Press.
Contributions of women in the physical and natural sciences and mathematics from prehistoric times to the last decade of the nineteenth century.

Allen, Gillian (1989). *Patron Response to Bibliographic Databases on CD-ROM.* Fall, 103-110. University of Illinois Library, Urbana, IL.
A study of library patron response to using CD-ROM databases. Allen found that while patrons like to use CD-ROMs, they are uncertain about their success in using the electronic system.

Atkinson, Steven and Judith Hudson (Eds.) (1990). *Women Online: Research in Women's Studies Using Online Databases.* New York: The Haworth Press.
This collection of innovative articles analyzes the coverage and content of on-line databases applicable to women's studies research published in the 1980s. Specific topics such as lesbian studies and women of color are also addressed.

Aumente, Jerome (1987). *New Electronic Pathways: Videotex, Teletext, and Online Databases.* Newbury Park: Sage.
This volume addresses the new era that has occurred with the convergence of telecommunications and computer technology (e.g., words are printed on the computer display screen for instant delivery to home or office; users can access information in the amount and sequence they wish, etc.). The book is a snapshot in time as individuals, groups, organizations, and corporations grapple with new information technologies. Overall, an informative but uncritical exploration.

Baker, Elizabeth (1964). *Technology and Woman's Work.* New York: Columbia University Press.
A somewhat dated but important work that traces the impact of technological advances on the lives of American women from the 18th century to the 1960s. The author calls it "a zigzag road in man's domain, beset with obstacles – social, economic, physical, and psychological."

Baran, Barbara (1985). "Office Automation and Women's Work: The Technological Transformation of the Insurance Industry." In Manuel Castells (Ed.), *High Technology, Space and Society* (pp. 143-171). Beverly Hills: Sage.
Study of the ways in which the insurance industry has been reorganized at the first stage of computer automation. Changes involve increased job fragmentation, narrowing of task functions, more centralized administration of workers, greater occupational sex segregation, and isolation of data entry from other clerical tasks.

Barr, Trevor (1985). *The Electronic Estate: New Communications Media and Australia.* Harmondsworth: Penguin Books.
The author argues that technology and communications policy in Australia have been characterized for decades by a profound neglect of social philosophy. Governments have lacked an integrated frame of reference for decision-making in the information technology fields, based on thorough social investigation, strategic planning, strong public awareness, and careful assessment of options for the future.

Barrett, Edward (Ed.) (1989). *The Society of Text: Hypertext, Hypermedia and the Social Construction of Information.* Cambridge: Massachusetts Institute of Technology Press.
A collection of academic essays in which the social implications of hypermedia and various forms of interactive technologies are considered.

Benston, Margaret Lowe (1982). "Feminism and the Critique of the Scientific Method." In A. Miles and G. Finn (Eds.), *Feminism in Canada* (pp. 47-66). Montreal: Black Rose Books.
A clear and well-written discussion that illuminates the gender biases in the dominant mode of scientific inquiry.

Bialo, Ellen and Jay Sivin (1990). *Report on the Effectiveness of Microcomputers in Schools.* Software Publishers Association.
This research review presents three reports on some of the positive news from recent educational technology research, focusing on the effects of microcomputers in education's effects on student achievement, student motivation, and social interaction in the learning environment. Very (almost suspiciously) pro-computer.

Bleier, Ruth (1984). *Science and Gender: A Critique of Biology and Its Theories on Women.* New York: Pergamon.
Bleier directs her attention primarily to biology and convincingly illustrates inherent masculine biases within the field.

Bleier, Ruth (1986). *Feminist Approaches to Science.* New York: Pergamon.
Bleier argues convincingly for the need for a feminist revision of science.

Boden, Margaret (1977). *Artificial Intelligence and Natural Man.* New York: Basic Books.
Boden suggests that as computers become increasingly commonplace, the human intelligence is defined as both like and unlike the information processing systems of computers. This redefinition may have consequences for a reconstruction of the meanings of feminine and masculine.

Bove, Tony and Cheryl Rhodes (1990). "New Publishing Tasks Migrating to the Desktop." *[Chicago] Tribune*, Section 19, 12.
Discussion of recent innovations in publishing. For instance, the desktop computer can be linked to professional production systems, blurring the distinctions between designer and production artist, writer and editor, and creative consultant and producer.

Bradley, Gunilla (1988). "Women, Work and Computers." *Women and Health*, 13(3-4), 117-132.
The introduction of computers into the working environment may raise fundamental issues about the organization of work, the working environment and other fundamental social and health issues. This paper delineates some of these social and health issues and describes governmental and private initiatives designed to understand them and to prevent potential adverse effects. In addition, results of an ongoing study of a research project, the RAM project, on computerization and the psychosocial environment of work are described. Based on these data, recommendations are made for future programs and actions designed to maximize worker health and well-being, with particular emphasis on women's roles and needs.

Brandin, David (1987). *The Technology War: A Case for Competitiveness.* New York: John Wiley and Sons.
This book presents an ambitious approach to the economic, sociological, educational and political factors in the international "race to capture the lead" in information technology. An alarmist, masculinist approach, conceptualizing the progress in technology as a "war" threatening U.S. dominance as a world power if it doesn't become more aggressively competitive with other countries (such as Japan).

Branscomb, Anne (1988). *Nurturing Creativity in a Competitive Global Economy: Intellectual Property and New Technologies.* Cambridge, Mass.: The Program on Information Resources Policy, Harvard University.
In this fascinating report, Anne Branscomb, a communications lawyer, assesses the status of intellectual property with respect to the impact of new information technologies by focusing on: 1) the inconsistencies in the various intellectual property systems; 2) identifying the challenges of established law from the impact of new information technologies; 3) locating forums in which discussions of public policy are taking place; 4) identifying targets of opportunity where action is needed to modify, reconcile, and harmonize the laws of the U.S. and other countries.

Brecher, Deborah (1985). *Women's Computer Literacy Handbook.* New York: Plume.
Based on the curriculum of the Women's Computer Literacy Project, which Deborah Brecher began in San Francisco in 1982, this volume provides readable, user-friendly practical information for women to gain computer skills without being patronized or paralyzed by unnecessary threats. Written for a true "nonuser."

Brighton Women in Science Group (Ed.) (1980). *Alice Through the Microscope: The Power of Science Over Women's Lives.* London: Virago Press.
A fine anthology focusing on the various ways in which science and technology have operated to control women. One part discusses the impact of science on women's bodies, and the other part discusses issues of women and technological control.

Brody, Herb (1991). "Great Expectations: Why Technology Predictions Go Awry." *Technology Review,* July, 38-44.
Brody provides some engaging examples of technological breakthroughs that never came to be, and discusses some of the economic, social, and political reasons for these faulty predictions.

Brunet, Jean and Serge Prouix (1989). "Formal Versus Grass-Roots Training: Women, Work and Computers." *Journal of Communication,* 39(3), 77-84.
This article describes and evaluates two types of microcomputer training programs – a series of private courses and training offered in Greater Montreal and an original training experiment by a Montreal neighborhood community group. The former is associated with formal training strategy, with traditional standards of schooling, while the latter involves grass-roots training for the "have-nots," who more often than not are women.

Bush, Corlann Gee (1983). "Women and the Assessment of Technology: To Think, To Be: To Unthink, To Free." In J. Rothschild (Ed.), *Machina Ex Dea: Feminist Perspectives on Technology* (pp. 151-170). New York: Pergamon.
Bush stresses the need for a feminist assessment of technology that takes into account the needs and wants of women.

Capek, Mary Ellen (1989). "Wired Worlds: Building a National and International On-line Thesaurus and Database for Access to Women's Information Resources." In Ramona Rush and Donna Allen (Eds.), *Communication at the Crossroads: The Gender Gap Connection* (pp. 208-221). Norwood, N.J.: Ablex.
Capek maintains that problems of access to important womens' texts are intimately linked to control of our cultural institutions and access to the media of access – publishing, newspaper and television coverage, libraries, microfilm contracts, periodical indexes, and computerized databases. Without this access to our own histories and equal access to the media, women lose the sustenance of our foremothers and each other. We are condemned again and again to start from scratch, to reinvent solutions to the same problems, to raise the same questions that repeat with enervating frequency in each new generation.

Cardman, Elizabeth (1990). "The Gender Gap in Computer Use: Implications for Bibliographic Instruction." *Research Strategies*, 8(3), 116-128.
Research in education and psychology has revealed a gender gap in the use of computers for which various explanations have been advanced. The ever-increasing automation of libraries makes it incumbent upon bibliographic instructors to address the probability that female populations of academic communities are at a disadvantage. Various nature-nurture studies are discussed in relation to this area, and further research is recommended.

Carlsson, C. (Ed.) (1990). *Bad Attitude: The Processed World Anthology*. New York: Verso.
A wonderful collection of the best articles, graphics, stories, poetry and cartoons from the magazine *Processed World*. Contributors cleverly and irreverently poke fun at the absurdity and alienation of work within the confines of bureaucratic corporate capitalism in the late 20th century. The magazine suffers, however, from a lack of sufficient awareness and discussion of the effects of gender, especially the experiences of women, in the workaday world. To its credit, the magazine aims at contributing to a grass-roots revolution by office workers everywhere.

Carnes, Alice and John Zerzan (Eds.) (1988). *Questioning Technology: A Critical Anthology*. London: Freedom Press.
Focuses on the history of technology, the adverse effect of industrial technology, and the myriad problems associated with the information society. The writers conclude with discussions of whether the regulation and control of science and technology is truly neutral or whether it has some autonomous force of its own. Included in this useful anthology is an essay by American Indian activist Russell Means, as well as the usual works by Mumford, Ellul, and computer critic Weizenbaum.

Chavkin, Wendy (Ed.) (1984). *Double Exposure: Women's Health on the Job and at Home*. New York: Monthly Review Press.
An excellent collection of essays critically exploring the ways in which new technologies affect the health and livelihood of women. Authors in the collection are not afraid to critique popular misconceptions of technology such as the fallacies of characterizing electronics manufacturing as a "clean" and "light" industry. As editor Wendy Chankin, M.D., writes, "[T]ime and again what we found was that [those in control thought] it was easier to exclude women than to clean up the workplace." This book takes a refreshingly activist stance. Good final chapter on grass-roots political organizing.

Chesterman, John and Arnold Lipman (Eds.) (1988). *The Electronic Pirates: DIY Crime of the Century*. London: Routledge.
This looks at the enormous scale of software piracy, in print, tapes, videos, and computer software. It uncovers the shady and dangerous world of electronic pirates, and its parallels with international drug dealing and terrorism.

Chivers, Geoffrey (Ed.) (1984). *Women in Technology*. Loughborough, England.
Proceedings of a conference held at Loughborough University in 1984. Papers deal with the subject of women in technology in three areas: work, school, and postschool and re-entry. The intent of the conference organizers was to bring the educational and industrial sectors together in a common discussion of U.K. activities and strategies to increase the participation of women in industry and technology.

Clark, B., M. Balachandran, S. Griffiths, P.McCandless, L. Wilson, and H. Bingham (1989). "Gender Gap in the Use of Library Technologies: Evidence, Implications and Intervention." In J. Fennell (Ed.), *Building on the First Century: Fifth National Conference of the Association of College and Research Libraries* (pp. 116-118). Cincinnati, Ohio.
Given the gender gap in the area of computer literacy, this paper explores libraries' increased use of computers to access information and poses the question of whether libraries are providing access biased toward males. Intervention strategies for addressing the gap are discussed.

Clark, J. (1987). "The American Image of Technology From the Revolution to 1840." *American Quarterly*, 39(3), 431-449.
This essay presents a historical analysis of the ways Americans saw, described, and intellectually dealt with new mechanical technology as a dynamic agent of change. The author does not describe the history of any particular machinery or process, but she focuses on the ideas which were evoked by the introduction of new technologies. More specifically, Clark examines the ways in which the idea of technology was expressed in nationalistic terms. Not much attention to gender.

Cockburn, Cynthia (1983). *Brothers: Male Dominance and Technological Change*. London: Pluto.
Cockburn focuses on the changes occurring in London's newspaper industry with the introduction of computer technology, and uses this example to explore the ways men use technology to maintain their patriarchal power.

Cockburn, Cynthia (1988). *Machinery of Dominance: Women, Men and Technical Know-How*. Boston: Northeastern University Press.
An examination of the effects of electronics technology on relations between employers and the relative positions of female and male workers. Comparisons between workplaces using traditional technologies and those using newer technologies are made. Studies were focused on the clothing industry, the mail-order industry, and the medical x-ray equipment industry.

Cohn, C (1987). "Sex and Death in the Rational World of Defense Intellectuals." *Signs*, 12, 687-718.
A fascinating ethnographic exploration of the language used by U.S. defense policy-makers. Cohn's analysis maintains that the deliberately dehumanizing terms used by policy-makers for war-related destruction of human life and property allows them to produce and deploy potentially apocalyptic weaponry.

Collins, Harry (1991). *Artificial Experts: Social Knowledge and Intelligent Machines*. Cambridge, Mass.: Massachusetts Institute of Technology Press.
Collins discusses the differences between human action and machine intelligence.

Cooper, Marilyn M. and Cynthia L. Selfe (1990). "Computer Conferences and Learning: Authority, Resistance, and Internally Persuasive Discourse." *College English*, 52(8): 847-869.
The authors argue that the biggest technology challenge for teachers is not more use of computers but the use of computers to make a real difference in classrooms. Although computer use cannot eliminate the effects of racism, sexism, and classism in classrooms, skillful planning may make possible smaller, reduced-risk, electronic spaces in which these problems can be acknowledged and debated.

Cottingham, Jane (1989). "ISIS: A Decade of International Networking," In R. Rush and D. Allen (Eds.), *Communication at the Crossroads: The Gender Gap Connection*. Norwood, N.J.: Ablex.
Cottingham documents the development of ISIS, an international bulletin quarterly, and discusses how the growth and success of the ISIS bulletin helped to foster the International Feminist Network. Although the networks discussed are not presently on line, the shared contacts exist for the translation to electronic linkages.

Cowan, Ruth Schwartz (1974). "A Case Study of Technological and Social Change: The Washing Machine and the Working Wife." In Mary Hartman and Lois W. Banter (Eds.), *Clio's Consciousness Raised*. New York: Harper Torch Books.
Cowan traces the introduction and use of a new technology, highlighting the ways in which the new technology altered the patterns of work and social relationships of the women who used it.

Cowan, Ruth Schwartz (1983). *More Work for Mother: The Ironies of Household Technology From the Open Hearth to the Microwave*. New York: Basic Books.
Through an examination of work processes and technological developments that have affected women's household work, the author traces changes that have occurred during the last hundred years.

Crawford, Stephen (1989). *Technical Workers in an Advanced Society: The Work, Careers and Politics of French Engineers*. New York: Cambridge University Press.
As Rudi Volti writes, "France may be considered the spiritual home of technocracy," because it was there the idea originated that those who possess technical expertise are best suited to hold the reins of power. Crawford addresses the validity of two popular and competing theories of technical expertise with respect to engineers. The first theory posits that postindustrial societies will be marked by the emergence of technical workers as a new economic and political elite, while the second theory posits that

engineers will continue to be subjected to systematic de-skilling along with decreases in their workplace responsibilities. Crawford's analysis of engineers in France supports neither the "technocratic" nor the "proletarianization" thesis. He found that, generally, French engineers have not suffered from de-skilling. Rather, they are often treated as valuable employees whose work continues to require high degrees of skill and responsibility. Yet, contrary to the technocratic thesis, they only assume roles of power when they leave engineering itself and take on management positions.

Cross, Anita and Robert McCormick (Eds.) (1986). *Technology in Schools: Exploring the Curriculum.* Milton Keynes: Open University Press.
This collection of readings (prepared by members of the Open University) explores what is increasingly being called technological education. The volume begins with grappling with defining technology, and then goes on to discuss the nature of technology, technology and human values, and technology and society. Issues of gender are addressed throughout.

Cubitt, S. (1991). *Timeshift: On Video Culture.* New York: Routledge.
Cubitt argues that video, as a new technological medium, is potentially democratic. Drawing upon various uses of video, such as video rental, off-air recording, music video, and video art, he valorizes the creative features available through video recording.

Dahms, Mona, Lone Dirckinck-Holmfeld, Kirsten Gronbaek Hansen, Anette Kolmos, and Janni Neilsen (1986). *Women Challenge Technology: Papers from a European Conference on Women, Natural Sciences and Technology.* Elsinore: Centertrykkeriet University Aalborg.
Collection of feminist perspectives on technology from the "Women Challenge Technology" conference.

Damarin, Suzanne K. (1986). "The Classroom of Tomorrow: The Challenge of Today." *Education Technology*, October, 23-28.
Considering possible conceptualizations for the classroom of the future, the author, who considers herself a "revolutionist," insists that technology will have a profound effect on all aspects of classroom management. The article details some of the author's predictions for the classroom of the future.

Damarin, Suzanne K. (1988). "Recontextualizing Computers in Education: A Response to Streibel." *Education, Communication and Technology Journal*, Fall, 147-152.
This article continues the discussion of educational computing begun by Streibel. The author focuses on contextualizing, from a broader view of computers in society, the use of computers in schools, making careful analysis of the power relationships involved.

Damarin, Suzanne K. (Ed.) (1990). *Unthinking Educational Technology.* Presented at the Seventh Annual Forum on Foundational Issues in Educational Technology, Association for Educational Communications and Technology. Anaheim, Calif.
A wonderfully lucid discussion of the ways in which educational technologies play a part in the reproduction of gender inequality. An especially good critique of the social scientific research methods which invariably produce a literature of gender "differences."

Damarin, Suzanne K. (1991). "Rethinking Science and Mathematics Curriculum and Instruction: Feminist Perspectives in the Computer Era." *Journal of Education*, 173-181.
Although the discussions of the gendered nature of science and scientific investigation have had a major impact on the conduct of educational research, the author maintains that there has been little written about how the issues raised in these discussions might or should affect the conduct of science education in schools. The purpose of this paper is to address this dearth of information with respect to the feminist analysis of science.

Dauber, Robert and Melinda L. Cain (Eds.) (1981). *Women and Technological Change in Developing Countries*. Boulder, Colo.: Westview Press.
Addresses the needs of women in adapting to technological change and as agents of that change. Considers the need for all components of society, women as well as men, to be involved in technological development if all are to benefit, and surveys the ways in which women are ignored and excluded through several case studies.

Davidson, Marilyn J. and Cynthia Cooper (Eds.) (1987). *Women and Information Technology*. New York: Wiley.
An investigation of the effect of new technology on women's employment and of the opportunities and problems that technology presents to women today and in the future. Divided into four sections: women and information technology: a cross-cultural perspective; information technology and women's employment in industry; information technology: the psychosocial effects and information technology and women; and new trends and initiatives.

de Jong, Frida (1989). "The Times, Are They A-Changin'?" In Kea Tijdens et al. (Eds.), *Women, Work and Computerization: Forming New Alliances* (pp. 105-115). North Holland: Elsevier Science Publishers.
The authors investigate how technology and stereotypes of women and technology repeatedly confirm the gendered division of labor. They describe the feminization of clerical work in the first half of the century in relation to the introduction of technical equipment in offices. Using Sullerot's theorizations as a point of reference, they compare this historical process with the current automation in the Netherlands.

de Sola Pool, Ithiel (1991). *Technologies Without Boundaries: On Telecommunications in a Global Age*. Cambridge, Mass.: Harvard University Press.
A compilation of several technological innovations in communication systems with a discussion of their effect on culture and society.

Delany, Paul (Ed.) (1991). *Hypermedia and Literary Studies*. Cambridge, Mass.: Harvard University Press.
The production of this anthology may well be of greater interest than its contents. The book began with a call for papers on an electronic network and communication among contributors occurred largely by means of e-mail and other networks. The manuscripts were submitted on disk, and the book layout was created through desktop publishing software. The focus of the volume is a discussion of hypertext and hypermedia for the literary classroom.

Dervin, Brenda, Lawrence Grossberg, Barbara J. O'Keefe, and Ellen Wartella (Eds.) (1989). *Rethinking Communication: Paradigm Exemplars.* Newbury Park, Calif.: Sage.
A collection of essays that address a variety of issues related to communication and technology from a speech communication perspective.

Detlefsen, E. G. (1986). "Issues of Access to Information About Women." In *Women's Collections.* New York: The Hayworth Press.
The author discusses five facets of issues of access to information for, by, and about women: 1) the distinction between information about women and feminist-informed information about women; 2) the necessity of an interdisciplinary approach; 3) problems posed for interdisciplinary work by the massive terminology and vocabulary used by different fields; 4) the inability to gain computer access to a great amount of information for and about women because much of this data remains only available in hard copy and in obscure indexes, and 5) the few projects that have surfaced to address the implications of #4 above.

Dillman, Don (1985). "The Social Impacts of Information Technologies in Rural North America." *Rural Sociology*, 50(1), 27-37.
Discussion of the effects of computer networks and other electronic media on the lives of rural women and men.

Doane, Mary Ann (1990). "Technophilia: Technology, Representation and the Feminine." In M. Jacobus et al. (Eds.), *Body/Politics: Women and the Discourses of Science* (pp. 163-176). New York: Routledge.
In this essay, Doane focuses on the intersection of technology, the body, and the question of sexual difference. She argues that anxiety about technology is usually displaced onto the figure of a woman or onto the idea of the feminine. Further, she argues that despite the emphasis in discourses about technology on the connection between the machine and production, the woman usually becomes the model of the perfect machine. She argues that, actually, it is not so much production that is at stake in such representations as it is reproduction.

(1989). *Documentation and Communication: Strategies for Networking and Change.* Isis-wicce, Isis-International, Network of Women Living Under Muslim Laws. (Report of conference of the same name, October 30-November 1, 1989, Geneva, Switzerland.)
This conference report focuses on the following areas of information distribution and networking: training, computerization and new technology, network strategies, and fund raising.

(1990). "Documentation and Communication: Strategies for Networking and Change." *Women's World*, 23.
This special issue of *Women's World* is inspired by the conference above, and it includes a multitude of conference-generated papers and reports, as well as several in-depth essays by staff members that focus on the necessity of providing women with access to documentation centers through informational networks.

Doniol-Shaw, Ghislaine (1989). "Technical Culture, Training and Female Employment." In Kea Tijdens et al. (Eds.), *Women, Work and Computerization: Forming New Alliances.* North Holland: Elsevier Science Publishers.
This paper, based on field-work done on blue-collar women and on training of women for highly technical, traditionally male vocations, questions the role played by technical culture in retraining on the entry or exclusion of women from certain types of jobs. The author argues that although the workplace is permeated with gendered power relations, technical culture should become a part of all kinds of training attended by women.

Donnelly, Denis. (Ed.) (1985). *The Computer Culture: A Symposium to Explore the Computer's Impact on Society.* Cranbury, N.J.: Associated University Presses.
An edited collection of essays on the cultural impact of new computer technologies that arose from the 1981 Computer Culture Symposium at Siena College. The book contains six essays and three question-and-answer sessions covering the two areas of artificial intelligence and computer influences in the sociopolitical realm. Unfortunately, however, all of the writers are male and the perspectives represented are uncritical. Ostensibly endeavoring to explore the social impact of computers, the writers fail to address such crucial social and political issues as gender, the "Third World," power, and de-skilling of labor. Instead, the social impact is assessed from the point of view of the white, Western, relatively privileged technologically literate male.

Dowling, C. (1980). *The Techno/Peasant Survival Manual.* New York: Bantam.
The author discusses the concept of techno/power – power that comes with the understanding and control over computer-information technology.

Dreyfus, Hubert (1986). "Computers in the Classroom: Tools, Tutors and Tutees: Mind Over Machine." In Herbert Dreyfus (Ed.) *The Power of Human Intuition and Expertise in the Era of the Computer.* New York: The Free Press.
This chapter seeks to expose the irresponsible uses of often inappropriate software in educational settings.

Dreyfus, Hubert (1979). *What Computers Can't Do: The Limits of Artificial Intelligence.* New York: Harper and Row.
In this somewhat dated work, Dreyfus questions the foundations of artificial intelligence. He appropriates a phenomenological approach and concludes that computers are limited not so much because they lack "minds" but "bodies."

Eames, Charles and Ray Eames (1991). *A Computer Perspective.* Cambridge, Mass: Harvard University Press.
History of the computer created by Charles and Ray Eames.

Easlea, Brian (1983). *Fathering the Unthinkable: Masculinity, Scientists and the Nuclear Arms Race.* London: Pluto.
Drawing upon feminist analyses of the development of science as a form of control of both nature and women, Easlea explains the creation of nuclear weapons in terms of the masculinity of science.

(1986) "Editorial." *Women's World: Appropriate Technology Issue,* December, 10.
Addresses the rationale behind the theme of this issue, appropriate technology. The editors of this feminist publication maintain that it is vitally important for women to become involved in policy-making decisions concerning technological deployment. With this agenda intact, this edition attempts to inform women about the historical, political and socioeconomic issues that affect the social deployment of various forms of technology.

Edwards, Paul N. (1990). "The Army and the Microworld: Computers and the Politics of Gender Identity." *Signs,* 16(1), 102-127.
Edwards' essay addresses the male-dominated cultural practices surrounding computer work. He suggests that in the U.S., the reasons behind the resulting inequities lie in the connections between the modes of thought involved in computer science research, the culture of engineering, and the deeply entangled institutions of military service and of masculinity as a political identity in an age of high technology war.

Ehrenreich, Barbara (1983).*Women in the Global Factory.* Boston: South End Press.
A discussion of the global assembly line in the electronics industry.

Ellul, Jacques (1980). *The Technological System.* New York: Seabury Continuum.
Ellul clarifies his notion of "autonomous technology." Drawing upon Marx's concept of alienation, the author suggests that technological systems are always self-augmenting, that they take on lives of their own. Today's technology "does not tolerate being halted for a moral reason."

Elson, Diane and Ruth Pearson (1981). "Nimble Fingers Make Cheap Workers: An Analysis of Women's Employment in Third World Manufacturing." *Feminist Review*, 7, 87-107.
Insightful look at the often erased work of women in high-technology production.

Ermann, David, Mary Williams, and Claudio Gutierrez (Eds.) (1990). *Computers, Ethics and Society.* New York: Oxford University Press.
The writers in this anthology discuss the moral problems caused by computers, focusing on how computer-related moral problems are approached and then on the potential effects of computers and the moral problems they generate. Issues addressed include an explication of ethical theory, privacy, quality of personal life, quality of work life, justice and the distribution of work, technology, and human freedom, as well as issues facing computer professionals.

Everett, Robert R. (1982). "Yesterday, Today and Tomorrow in Command, Control and Communications." *Technology Review,* January, 66-68.
This article explores the impact of new information technologies on U.S. military communications.

Faulkner, Wendy and Erik Arnold (Eds.) (1985). *Smothered By Invention: Technology in Women's Lives.* London: Pluto Press.
Explores the questions of technology as it relates to women, male control of and the exclusion of women from technology, and the relationship between contemporary technology and oppression. Topics include birth control, medical technology, the Green Revolution, kitchen technology, and computers.

Fausto-Sterling, Anne (1981). "Women and Science." *Womens' Studies International Quarterly*, 4(1), 41-50.
An informative survey of women in science-based educational programs and careers.

Fedorick, J. A. (1989). "Mother Tongue: Aboriginal Cultures and Languages." *Native Woman,* 10(2 & 3), 69-70.
This article considers the importance of language and education in reclaiming the native cultures that dominant white society has attempted to malign and colonize. In an attempt to address the needs of nomadic and isolated Native American artists, the Earthtones North project was designed. The project combines methodologies of professional development, networking, enhancement of public profile, and experimental group productions, using as its foundation applications of computer technology and media communications. The article details project objectives as well as successes with its specific applications.

Feldberg, Roslyn and Evelyn Nakano Glenn (1988). "Technology and Work Degradation: Effects of Office Automation on Women Clerical Workers." In Joan Rothschild (Ed.), *Teaching Technology from a Feminist Perspective: A Practical Guide* (pp. 59-78). New York: Pergamon.
Discussion of the ways in which the introduction of new information technologies contributed to the de-skilling and feminization of office work.

Ferguson, Edward S. (1968). *Bibliography of the History of Technology.* Cambridge, Mass.: Massachusetts Institute of Technology Press.
Compilation of key texts and monographs that record the various phases of technological development and proliferation in the West.

Fersko-Weiss, H. (1985). "Electronic Mail: The Emerging Connection." *Personal Computing,* 9: 71-79.
Discussion of the ways in which electronic mail allows users to expand their perceptual horizons by tapping into library data and bibliographic information. The author also stresses the potential of the electronic medium to enhance the user's knowledge of individuals from other cultures and countries.

Finnegan, Ruth (1989). "Communication and Technology." *Language and Communication,* 9(2/3), 107-127.
This paper addresses the significance of a historical approach to technology, using Walter Ong's work on "transformation of the word" to situate current technological innovations and practices. The author then offers some more general implications for the analysis of transformations of the word for communication scholars.

Florman, Samuel C. (1976). *The Existential Pleasures of Engineering.* New York: St. Martin's Press.
Discussion of the joys of learning, performing under pressure, and making things work in an engineering context.

Florman, Samuel C. (1988). "Liberating Technologies." *Technology Review*, October, 18.
The author, citing specific examples of technology used to subvert dictatorial regimes, maintains that new communication technologies are expanding freedom of information around the world. A rabid pro-technology position.

Fulk, Jerome (Ed.) (1990). *Organizations and Communication Technology.* Newbury Park, Calif.: Sage.
These contributors generate empiricist essays about the interface of organization and communication technology. Each addresses one or more of the following questions: What forces shape the articulation of organizational and technological systems? What organizational, political, and social processes constrain technological possibilities? Unfortunately, virtually all of these essays ignore gender.

Garson, Barbara (1988). *The Electronic Sweatshop: How Computers Are Transforming the Office of the Future Into the Factory of the Past.* New York: Simon and Schuster.
In this volume, Barbara Garson follows white-collar automation up the occupational ladder from the prototypes – fast-food burger-flipper and airline reservation clerk – to the stockbroker, the executive, and the admiral, as representatives from each occupation describe their feelings toward having their job automated. Garson asserts that the combination of 20th century technology and 19th century scientific management is turning the office of the future into the factory of the past.

Gay, G. and Raffensperger, E. (1989). "Considerations and Strategies in the Design of Interactive Multimedia Programs." *Academic Computing*, September, 24-25, 57-58.
Discusses the use of interactive media and Hypercard for instructional purposes.

Glendinning, Chellis (1990). *When Technology Wounds: The Human Consequences of Progress.* New York: William Morrow and Company, Inc.
Glendinning writes a compelling book about technology survivors. Having documented hundreds of people's stories about their experiences with the threats of modern technologies, the author warns us that the fact that our technologies so uniformly threaten health and life is no coincidence – their development originates in a philosophical and political approach to life.

Glenn, E. M. and R. L. Feldberg (1977). "Degraded and Deskilled: The Proletarianization of Clerical Work." *Social Problems*, 25, 52-64.
Discussion of the effects of the deployment of new information technologies on office work.

Global Electronics (1991). "Bombay Women Organize," *Global Electronics,* 111, Mountain View, Calif.: Pacific Studies Center.
Discussion of the attempts of electronic assembly workers, 90% of whom are women, to unionize at the Santacruz Electronics Export Processing Zone in Bombay. Since 1984, workers at several plants have tried to organize, but employers, with the help of police, have systematically suppressed those efforts.

Goldstine, Herman Heine (1972). *The Computer from Pascal to von Neumann.* Princeton, N.J.: Princeton University Press.
Goldstine participated in the development and design of the Electronic Numerical Integrator and Computer (ENIAC). In this book he recounts its history while stressing the controversial link between universities and the military.

Gonick, Larry (1983). *The Cartoon Guide to Computer Science.* New York: Harper and Row.
This illustrated guide introduces the novice to computer science by employing the nonthreatening conventions of cartoon drawings and captions. Contents include a discussion of information, the information age, computer hardware, and software.

GRANITE (Ed.) (1990). *For Business Only: Gender and New Information Technologies.* Amsterdam: SISWO.
A collection of selected papers from the first colloquium of the international network GRANITE (Gender and New Information Technologies) in Amsterdam in 1990. The network aims at increasing knowledge and improving policy about gender and new interactive media. Topics addressed include research on gender and new information technologies, information technology development and impact on everyday life, and women and new technologies. GRANITE also produces a newsletter.

Griffiths, Dorothy (1985). "The Exclusion of Women From Technology." In Wendy Faulkner and Erik Arnold (Eds.), *Smothered by Invention: Technology in Women's Lives* (pp. 51-71). London: Pluto Press.
The author, an instructor at the University of London, examines the exclusionary practices with respect to technology at her institution to address the following questions: Why are there so few women in technology in Britain? How are women excluded from technology? What implications does this exclusion have for women's experience of and relationship with technology?

Griffiths, Morwena (1988). "Strong Feelings About Computers." *Womens' Studies International Forum*, 11(2), 145-154.
Given that women are increasingly absent from the world of computers, Griffiths asserts that the reasons for this are related to the way computers have become associated with technology – and technology with masculinity. Griffiths examines the lack of logic in the association of technology with masculinity, and argues that women need to subvert this false articulation and create an alternative vision.

Grosz, Elizabeth (1989). "Writing Our Way Into the Picture: Women in the Technological Arts." ***Refractory Girl*****, May, 17-19.**
This paper discusses the author's work in the areas of language and representational systems, of understanding women's unique contributions to the study of knowledges, and ways of extending these contributions to the area of cinema and video production.

Grunwald, Joseph and K. Flamm (1985). ***The Global Factory: Foreign Assembly in International Trade.*** **Washington, D.C.: The Brookings Institution.**
The authors examine industrial collaboration between developed and developing countries, focusing on the transfer of assembly operations abroad. In particular, they analyze those activities that involve the U.S. with Mexico, Haiti, and Colombia, considering in detail the worldwide production in the semiconductor industry.

Gunn, Angela (1991). "Computer Bulletin Boards Not Just Boy Toy." ***New Directions for Women*****, November-December, 7.**
Presents some general information about the potential benefits of computer bulletin boards systems (BBS) for women. Although there are over 40,000 BBSs in the world, women make up only 5% of their users.

Gustavsson, B. (Ed.) (1985). ***Work in the 1980s: Emancipation and Derogation.*** **London: Gower.**
This volume presents the proceedings of the Karlstad Symposium on Work, held at the University of Karlstad, Sweden, on June 17-20, 1984. In the essays, the contributors go beyond a mere description and analysis of the problems of work and into worthwhile discussions of various ways of achieving emancipation.

Hacker, Sally (1989). ***Power, Pleasure and Technology: Some Tales of Gender, Engineering and the Cooperative Workplace.*** **Winchester, Mass.: Unwin Hyman.**
This book first describes the pleasures of growing up with technology as a natural part of life, then suggests that we have gendered that pleasure, which affects both social structure and the shape of technology.

Hacker, Sally (1990). ***Doing It the Hard Way: Investigations of Gender and Technology.*** **Boston: Unwin Hyman.**
The material in this useful volume is drawn from discussions between Dorothy Smith and Sally Hacker in which Hacker explicates her analysis of the intersections between gender, power, and technology. Topics discussed include Hacker's critical method, women, technology and the corporations, gender and the culture of technology, technological change and the changing stratification of engineering, and sexuality and technology.

Haraway, Donna (1985). "A Manifesto for Cyborgs: Science, Technology, and Socialist Feminism in the 1980s." ***Socialist Review*****, 15:2.**
Haraway presents her provocative concept of cyborgs to illustrate that there is no essential women or an organic wholeness to prior to patriarchal violation. She argues that women should embrace the possibilities of technology for radical social change and proposes not a "Goddess" but a "cyborg"– a fusion of human, animal, and machine – as a preferred mythic identity for women.

Haraway, Donna (1989). ***Primate Visions: Gender, Race and Nature in the World of Modern Science.*** **New York: Routledge.**
A collection of her essays, which represent an important cultural studies approach to technology.

Hardison, O. B. Jr. (1989). ***Disappearing Through the Skylight: Culture and Technology in the Twentieth Century.*** **New York: Viking.**
Hardison, a cultural critic, attempts to trace the ways culture has changed in the past century, changing the identities of "all born into it." Hardison maintains that the universalizing process of technology, a cornerstone of modern times, has caused us (Westerners, although he doesn't specify) to lose our individuality. Although somewhat self-indulgent and embarrassingly ignorant of non-Western cultures, the author does offer an interesting and lucid approach to the ways in which various cultural forms have been altered by new technologies.

Hayes, Dennis (1989). ***Behind the Silicon Curtain: The Seductions of Work in a Lonely Era.*** **Boston: South End Press.**
This disturbing account of the underside of Silicon Valley provides a much-needed antidote to the promises of zealous advocates of the computer age.

Heath, Deborah (1991). "Computers and Their Bodies: Sex, War and Cyberspace." Unpublished paper. Portland, Ore.: Lewis and Clark College.
Discussion of the nexus of gender, computers, and the ever-shifting boundaries between body and machine. The author perceives the representations of women in computer advertisements as dangerous cyborgs and argues for a recontexualization of the cyborg concept in order to foster more egalitarian cyborgs in the future.

Herring, Susan D. (1989). ***From the Titanic to the Challenger: An Annotated Bibliography on Technological Failures of the Twentieth Century.*** **New York: Garland.**
This annotated bibliography provides a good beginning for the disaster researcher. Susan Herring provides 1,354 well-indexed entries on the best-known engineering failures of the 20th century. The focus is on technological failures caused by poor design, such as airplane crashes, as opposed to technological failures caused by natural disasters, such as earthquakes. Sections include engineering ethics, predisaster coverage, and the notion of chronic, as opposed to discrete, technological failure.

Hohn, Hubert (1988). "The Art of a New Machine, or Confessions of a Computer Artist." ***Technology Review,*** **November/December , 64-73.**
The author, a computer artist and director of the Computer Arts Learning Center at the Massachusetts College of Art, discusses how his work explores a computer aesthetic based on the unique properties of the machine.

Horvath, A. T. (1991). "Attitudes Toward Technological Systems: A Preliminary Investigation." Presented at the International Communication Association Annual Conference: Chicago, Illinois, May.
This empiricist-based study attempts to explore the structure of attitudes toward technological systems, locating this inquiry within a larger framework of the social meaning of technology. This paper seeks to contribute to a theoretical and methodological

framework for research on the psychological, social, and technological bases of human attitudes toward technological processes. Unfortunately, gender is ignored.

Huws, Ursula (1985). "Terminal Isolation: The Atomisation of Work and Leisure in the Wired Society." ***Radical Science*, 16, 7-26.**
This article examines recent developments in information technologies to look at the growing importance of the home as the locus of profound shifts in the boundaries between what is "public" and what is "private." Huws also discusses some of the effects of information technology on the home, arguing that in some cases it provides the means whereby women workers are returned to the home and to the domination of husbands, without the loss of their services as cheap forms of labor.

(1986) "If It's Not Appropriate for Women, It's Not Appropriate." ***Women's World*, December, 15-16.**
Critiques the current AT movement for ignoring womens' needs, desires and concerns and maintains that the promise of AT willl remain unfulfilled until underlying, often gendered, power imbalances are challenged.

(1986). "Introduction." ***Women's World*, December, 3-5.**
Describes the history of appropriate technology movements in the west. Also details the current goal of practicing appropriate technology, emphasizing the importance of meeting basic human needs while fostering self-reliance and building a sustainable society. Appropriate technology attempts to offer an alternative path of development while seriously questioning the meaning of various related concepts such as "progress," "economic growth," "development," and "desirable standards of living."

Jacobson, F. (1991). "Gender Differences in Attitudes Toward Using Computers in Libraries: An Exploratory Study." ***Library and Information Science Research*, 13(3), 267-279.**
This article discusses the results of a study of 40 academically oriented high-school students, analyzing data about sex differences in library anxiety, computer anxiety, and anxiety about using computers for research. The research suggests that by placing computers in a "nonmathematical" educational setting, females may experience less computer anxiety but that the negativity associated with computers may compromise females' attitudes about the computer mediated activities that they engage in

Jain, Sugan Chand (Ed.) (1985). ***Women and Technology*. Jaipur: Rawat Publications.**
A series of essays that examines the impact of technology on women in India. Authors look at the drudgery experienced by women in a variety of traditional occupations and at their displacement by male workers when particularly onerous operations are mechanized or automated. Increased participation of women in the development process is advocated.

Jansen, Sue Curry (1988). "The Ghost in the Machine: Artificial Intelligence and Gendered Thought Patterns." *Resources for Feminist Research*, 17(4), 4-7.
Adopting a constructivist-informed feminist sociology of science that maintains that women's exclusion from the conversations of Western science has generated an incomplete and single-minded body of knowledge, Jansen explores notions of artificial intelligence. Her work asserts that the masculinization of logical-mathematical competencies has been reified by the structures, rules, paradigms, models, and methodologies of contemporary science. By undertaking a case study of the language, models, and disciplinary assumptions of the science of artificial intelligence, Jansen seeks to enable wider participation in the conversations of contemporary science.

Jennings, Kelly (1990). *The Devouring Fungus: Tales of the Computer Age.* New York: W. W. Norton.
A collection of amusing computer lore that focuses on the masculine culture and mythology of computing.

Joerges, Berward (1990). "Images of Technology in Sociology: Computer as Butterfly and Bat." *Technology and Culture,* 31(2), 203-227.
The author writes about the power of metaphors to structure experience, with the discussion focusing on the uncertain role of metaphors for technology in the professional talk of sociologists.

Johnson, Deborah G. (1985). *Computer Ethics.* Englewood Cliffs, N.J.: Prentice-Hall.
A well-written book by Deborah G. Johnson, chair of the Committee on Computers and Philosophy of the American Philosophical Association. Johnson argues that the "computer culture" poses a different context for age-old ethical quandaries. She begins with a general discussion of ethical theory, and then moves to more specific discussions of computers and power, computers and privacy, the ownership of computer programs, and professional ethics. Useful readings are suggested at the end of each chapter. The main weakness of the book, however, is its failure to take gender into consideration. (This book is one in the series of books on occupational ethics. Also included in the series are books on business ethics, medical ethics, ethics in government, and ethics in the practice of psychology.)

Jonas, Hans (1984). *The Imperative of Responsibility: In Search of an Ethics for the Technological Age.* Chicago: University of Chicago Press.
The author asserts that today's technological developments demand an entirely new ethics: "Modern technology has introduced actions of such novel scale, objects, and consequences that the framework of former ethics can no longer contain them."

Kamel, Rachel (1990). *The Global Factory: Analysis and Action for a New Economic Era.* New York: Omega Press.
The American Friends Service Committee's dedication to subverting systems of oppression and worker exploitation is chronicled in this work, which also seeks to explain the causes and results of exploitation on a global level. This guide provides useful information on organizing educational and action-oriented programs for the factory workers, and includes a comprehensive international list of organizations and references.

Karpf, Anne (1987). "Recent Feminist Approaches to Women and Technology." In Maureen McNeil (Ed.), *Gender and Expertise* (pp. 158-170). London: Free Association Books.
Lucid discussion of ways in which the nexus of gender and technology has been conceptualized. Shortcomings of some theorizations are highlighted and suggestions for further development given.

Katz, A. and K. Myers (1986). "Who Controls AT? Identifying the Economic Obstacles." *Women's World,* December, 23-27.
This article presents a critical analysis of the economic issues surrounding appropriate technology in industrialized countries. As appropriate technology is appropriated into existing international financial and commercial structures, which have been far from beneficial to most women, the result for women will continue to be, at best, their insertion into the economy as low-paid workers or, at worst, their further marginalization and impoverishment.

Keller, Evelyn Fox (1985). *Reflections on Gender and Science.* New Haven: Yale University Press.
Keller discusses the nature of Western scientific knowledge from its Baconian inception to its current practice and untangles the twisted strands of masculine and scientific ideology, using examples of concrete practice in biology and physics.

Kiesler, Sara, Lee Sproull, and Jacqueline S.Eccles (1985). "Poolhalls, Chips and War Games: Women in the Culture of Computing." *Psychology of Women Quarterly,* 9(4), 451-462.
Discussion of the dominant culture of computer games, which valorizes competition and war games.

Kiesler, Sara and Lee Sproull (Eds.) (1987). *Computing and Change on Campus.* Cambridge: Cambridge University Press.
This book aims to improve our understanding of what computers mean for organizations by presenting a collection of systematic research studies of the computerization of one university.

Klapp, Orrin Edgar (Ed.) (1986). *Overload and Boredom: Essays on the Quality of Life in the Information Society.* Westport, Conn.: Greenwood Press.
Klapp takes a Luddite view toward technology, asserting that boredom is one of the prime results of technology in the workplace. He moves from this premise to theorize about "the degradation of information and the increasing entropy of modern science" despite, and to some extent on account of, its large information load.

Knorr-Cetina, Karin D. (1981). *The Manufacture of Knowledge: An Essay on the Constructivist and Contextual Nature of Science.* New York: Pergamon.
Already a classic in the sociology of knowledge, this volume explicates the social and cultural contingencies within which the making of science and knowledge occurs. Though not an overtly feminist book, the arguments in this volume are ripe for feminist appropriation.

Korvjarvi, Paivi (1989). "New Technology and Gendered Division of Labor." In Kea Tijdens et al. (Eds.), *Women, Work and Computerization: Forming New Alliances* (pp. 77-83). North Holland: Elsevier Science Publishers.
The author focuses on the strictly gendered job segregation in Finland, suggesting that empirical studies on clerical workers ignore the hierarchic organizational structures that are the strongest obstacles to female clerical workers' use of a new technology and improving their positions within an organization. Current research, the article maintains, should focus less on technology and its impacts as such, but more on the the gender system and its cultural features in the structures of wage labor.

Kramarae, Cheris (Ed.) (1988). *Technology and Women's Voices: Keeping in Touch.* New York: Routledge and Kegan Paul.
This collection of essays on women and technology contributes to communication and gender research, and serves as a challenge and invitation to malestream researchers to question the assumption that men in the West have a location that is separate and adequate for theorizing about communication and technology. Topics addressed in the volume include women and computers, telephones, typewriters, and printing as well as sewing machines, washing machines, and microphones.

Kramer, Pamela E. and Sheila Lehman (1990). "Mismeasuring Women: A Critique of Research on Computer Ability and Avoidance." *Signs*, 16(1), 158-172.
This article maintains that although gender-related differences in learning and using computers can be documented at all educational levels, their causes are often unclear. In an attempt to clarify these ambiguities, the authors analyze the mainstream's biases and assumptions toward studying women and technology.

Kraut, Robert and Louise Tilly (1986). *Computer Chips and Paper Clips: Technology and Women's Development* (vol. 1). Washington, D.C.: National Academy Press.
Report of the Panel on Technology and Women's Employment.

Krohn, R. (1971). *The Social Shape of Science: Institutions, Ideology and Careers in Science.* Westport, Conn.: Greenwood Publishing Corporation.
Report on the author's research comparing and contrasting the attitudes and conceptions among scientists in various contexts, including university, government, and industry.

LaFrance, Marianne (1991). "Computers as Barrier or Vehicle to Equity." Paper presented to the National Conference on Computing and Values, New Haven, Conn., July.
This article responds to Walter Maner's paradigmatic assertion that access to information is a basic human right, arguing that Maner's analysis fails to consider the systemic inequalities that computers often reinforce.

Langley-Levy Moore, Doris (1977). *Ada, Countess of Lovelace: Byron's Legitimate Daughter.* London: J. Murray.
Biography of Ada Lovelace, the woman who introduced the binary system of computer programming. [The Department of Defense has named its newest computer language ADA in Lovelace's honor.]

Lawrence, John Shelton (1984). ***The Electronic Scholar: A Guide to Academic Microcomputing.*** **Norwood, N.J.: Ablex.**
A particularly uncritical yet informative discussion of computer applications relevant to academic microcomputing. The author covers topics such as cooperative writing and revision, electronics and publication, electronic filing, and legal and social issues. Some sections are outdated, such as those on word processing and electronic searches for information. The author's virtually unqualified embracement of computer technology is worrisome, however, and his class bias is clear when he writes that "once popularized, the idea of personal computing led to a variety of brands, operating systems, and inexpensive programs, now available to ordinary people from every station in life" (p166). The book concludes with naive optimism for a future in which the academic environment will be characterized by "computopia."

Lehto, A. M. (1989). "Women's Labour Market Position From the Perspective of Technological Change." In Kea Tijdens et al. (Eds.), ***Women, Work and Computerization: Forming New Alliances*** **(pp. 95-104). North Holland: Elsevier Science Publishers.**
A recent extensive interview survey carried out in Finland has studied the spread of new information technology and its effects on employment and on job content. This survey, as well as statistical information on labour, informs this paper, which considers the position of women active in different sectors of the economy with respect to technological change.

Leinback, Thomas (Ed.) (1991). ***Collapsing Space and Time: Geographic Aspects of Communication and Information.*** **London: Harper Collins Academic.**
This collection of essays addresses the recent changes in the world's economic and political map. Authors discuss the ways in which communications on a global scale shape the way we think and behave as individuals, members of communities and organizations, and as states. They argue that these changes are also apparent in the spatial patterns in organization, behavior, interaction, and decision-making.

Lemonick, Michael D. (1991). "Erotic Electronic Encounters." ***Time*****, Sept., 23.**
This article describes, in titillating journalistic detail, the latest form of pornography available to consumers: software porn games.

Levidow, Les (1991). "Women Who Make the Chips." ***Science as Culture*****, 2, part 1(10), 103-124.**
A study of the lives of the women of Malaysia who labor in the microelectronics firms. The author stresses the great human costs that remain largely hidden to all who use microelectronic devices.

Lewis, Linda H. (1987). "Females and Computers: Fostering Involvement." In Barbara Drygulski Wright et al. (Eds.), ***Women, Work and Technology: Transformations*** **(pp. 268-280). Ann Arbor: University of Michigan Press.**
This article examines a variety of factors that contribute to disparities in computer use and participation and suggests ways for developing sex equity in computer education and training. The author examines environmental variables, such as classroom interactions, and incorrect assumptions about the mathematical basis of computers that act to inhibit female participation.

Linn, Pam (1987). "Gender Stereotypes, Technology Stereotypes." In Maureen McNeil (Ed.), *Gender and Expertise* (pp. 127-151). London: Free Association Books.
This essay deconstructs popular empiricist approaches to understanding the "hardware" of technology. Linn first discusses definitions of technological practice from a class perspective, and then from a gender perspective, finally describing the difficulties encountered in generating a practical definition of technology.

Lippitt, Jill (1988). "The Feminist Face of Computer Technology." *Women of Power*, 11, 56-57.
The author maintains that just because technology is a product of patriarchal social relations, this relationship does not guarantee an essential male bias. Patriarchy, according to Lippitt, did not create technology. Rather, patriarchy exploited and distorted it from its original beginnings during the ascendancy of matristic cultures. The author maintains that in order for women to become more comfortable with technology, we need to first understand its female roots and then approach technology from a more holistic perspective.

Lloyd, Anne and Liz Newell (1985). "Women and Computers." In Wendy Faulkner and Erik Arnold (Eds.), *Smothered by Invention: Technology in Women's Lives* (pp. 238-251). London: Pluto Press.
A brief overview of the recent history of the work and experiences of women involved in computing.

Lovejoy, Margot (1989). *Postmodern Currents: Art and Artists in the Age of Electronic Media*. Ann Arbor: University of Michigan Research Press.
Lovejoy discusses three electronic media – video, computers, and photocopiers – and the effect they have had as artists have increasingly woven them into their works. Electronic technologies have become valuable tools to artists and have helped to foster new art forms in addition to shaping alternative meanings of what constitutes "art" itself.

Luke, Timothy (1987). *Screens of Power: Ideology, Domination, and Resistance in Informational Society*. Urbana: University of Illinois Press.
Drawing on the critical philosophies of the Frankfurt School, Luke explores the ways in which power operates within the relatively new material conditions of information based societies. He argues that the process of informationalization is not moving forward without resistance. Rather, it is being met by various social, cultural and economic forms of resistance that challenge the social order prescribed by informationalization.

Lyon, David (1987). "Hey You! Make Way for My Technology!" *Technology Review*, August/September, 28-29.
The author maintains that the instrumental and anonymous nature of consumer technology has encouraged the development of a more thoughtless and self-centered society.

MacKenzie, Donald and Judy Wajcman (Eds.) (1985). *The Social Shaping of Technology*. Philadelphia: Open University Press.
An excellent collection of essays about the ways in which technologies – domestic, military, and productive – are shaped by social forces. Particular attention is given to the interactions and contradictions between capitalism and patriarchy.

Madison, Mary Ann and Vary T. Coates (1989). "Women, Work and Technology: The Labour Market." In Kea Tijdens et al. (Eds.), *Women, Work and Computerization: Forming New Alliances* (pp. 85-93). North Holland: Elsevier Science Publishers.
This essay builds from the fact that employment levels and occupational choices for women have been heavily dependent on national economic performance, demographics, and social/cultural environments, and new technologies are adding another dimension to the impacts of these jobs. The authors predict areas of growth for women's employment opportunities, concluding that although technical and information-oriented jobs will show large increases in percent of new jobs, actual numbers of jobs will decrease.

Manacorda, Paola, Miriam Bergamaschi, and Clelia Bertello (1989). "Using Computers in the Interests of Women: An Equal Opportunity Information System." In Kea Tijdens et al. (Eds.), *Women, Work and Computerization: Forming New Alliances* (pp. 283-288). North Holland: Elsevier Science Publishers.
This paper describes an Italian Equal Opportunity Information System designed within a vocational training course for Equal Opportunities Advisers, most of them women.

Martin, Michele (1989). " 'Rulers of the Wires'? Women's Contributions to the Structure and Means of Communication." *Journal of Communication Inquiry*, Spring, 89-103.
This historical study examines the way in which the telephone was related to women as workers and homemakers. The first part examines women, primarily from low-income classes, as producers and then as consumers, mostly belonging to the bourgeoisie.The second part considers the dialectical relationship between women and telephone use, namely the contribution of women to the structure of the telephone as well as the impact of the telephone on these women's cultural practices. The study itself is an attempt to bridge the gap between political economy study and a feminist analysis of the development of an interactive means of communication.

Mattelart, A. (1985). *Communication and Information Technologies: Freedom of Choice for Latin America?* Norwood, N.J.: Ablex.
This book analyzes the evolution of communication and information systems as a global system for the organization of power, but also as a system where various social, cultural, and industrial projects confront one another.

McGaw, Judith (1982). "Women and the History of American Technology." *Signs*, 7(4), 798-828.
This article reviews recent progress made by feminist scholars in the following areas: technology's impingement on women's activities as bearers and rearers of children; technology's relationship to the segregated and exploitative world of women's employment; technology's role in the home; and technology's relationship to women's education.

McLuhan, Marshall (1951). *The Mechanical Bride: Folklore of Industrial Man.* Boston: Beacon.
A classic text in mass communication theory.

McNeil, Maureen (Ed.) (1987). *Gender and Expertise.* London: Free Association Books.
McNeil's chapter in this collection, a review of Cynthia Cockburn's book, *Machinery of Dominance,* considers how Cockburn's work builds on and challenges some of the parameters of Marx's and Engel's perspectives on the sexual division of labor.

Mehan, Hugh (1989). "Microcomputers in Classrooms: Educational Technology or Social Practice?" *Anthropology and Education Quarterly,* 20, 4-22.
This paper is the report of a year-long study of the effects of computers in four elementary school classrooms. The author insists that confusing technology with social practice will not yield useful information about computers in education, and that we must recognize that computers are always part of a larger social system in order to see the mutually influential relationship between classroom organization and computer use.

Merchant, Carolyn (1980). *The Death of Nature: Women, Ecology and the Scientific Revolution.* San Francisco: Harper and Row.
A historical analysis of Western technological innovations and their effects on women and nature.

Meyrowitz, Joshua (1985). *No Sense of Place: The Impact of Electronic Media on Social Behavior.* New York: Oxford University Press.
The situational analysis offered here describes how electronic media affect social behavior – not through the power of their messages but by reorganizing the social settings in which people interact and by weakening the once strong relationship between physical place and social "place." The study shows how, as we lose our old sense of place, we gain new notions of appropriate social behavior and identity.

Microsyster (1988). *Not Over Our Heads: Women and Computers in the Office.* (Report of the conference of the same name, March 28 -29, 1987, London.) London: Microsyster.
Microsyster, a feminist computer collective established in 1982 to provide computing services to women and womens' groups, sponsored this conference, the purpose of which was to present a space for more than 500 women office workers to converge and discuss issues related to the automation of their offices. Questions raised and discussed in this text include how computers are altering women's office work, how computers are changing job opportunities for women, how computers change the nature of office work, and who benefits from automation.

Miles, Ian (1988). *Home Informatics: Transformation Technology and the Transformation of Everyday Life.* New York: Pinter.
This book sets out a view of the dynamics of technological development, consumer behavior, and industrial strategies to illuminate future forms and implications of information technologies used by members of private households.

Morgall, Janine Marie (1991). ***Developing Technology Assessment – A Critical Feminist Approach.*** **Copenhagen: Stougaard Jensen.**
Technology assessment (TA) and medical technology assessment (MTA) are gaining in importance and are currently developing as instruments for exercising political and social control over existing as well as future forms of technology. This book examines the potential and limitations of TA and MTA in an attempt to develop a critical feminist approach to TA.

Morgall, Janine Marie (1991). ***Developing Technology Assessment – A Critical Feminist Approach.*** **Copenhagen: Stougaard Jensen.**
In this wonderfully lucid book, Morgall examines the relationship between technological change and the potential for either liberation or control in women's lives. She focuses on technological assessment, discussing its historical evolution, methods, and institutional organization problems; then she turns to the discussion of a feminist perspective on technology assessment, drawing upon the work of Corleen Gee Bush and Patricia Hynes. She goes on to discuss the key theoretical considerations and methods of a feminist-informed approach to technology assessment.

Mosco, Vincent (1989). ***The Pay-per Society: Computers and Communication in the Information Age.*** **Norwood, N.J.: Ablex.**
Mosco describes the ways in which information and information technology play a key role in the social and economic processes of commodification and control. His critically based analysis of computers in the information society includes discussions of information as commodity, information as resource, information as a means of social control, and information as a discourse on technology.

Mosco, Vincent (1989). "Labor in Communication Industries: A Critical Sociological Perspective." In Brenda Dervin, Lawrence Grossberg, Barbara J. O'Keefe, and Ellen Wartella (Eds.), ***Rethinking Communication: Paradigm Exemplars.*** **Newbury Park: Sage.**
Mosco attempts to understand the effects of changes in technology on society by using a critical sociological paradigm. This chapter focuses on the role of work and working people within the rapidly changing communication and computer industries.

Mosco, Vincent and Jane Wasko (Eds.) (1988). ***The Political Economy of Information.*** **Madison: University of Wisconsin Press.**
The essays in this book address the theoretical significance of information, the specific domains in which the roles and consequences of a political economy are revealed, and internationally inflected perspectives on the political economy of information.

Moskin, Robert (1989). ***Toward the Year 2000: New Forces in Publishing.*** **Jerusalem International Book Fair, The Aspen Institute, Bertelsmann Foundation.**
This report focuses on how book publishing will be changed by new communication technologies (e.g., hypermedia, desktop publishing), and by new conglomerates and multinational corporations that make up the industry.

Mulgan, Gerrald (1991). *Communication and Control: Networks and the New Economics of Communication.* New York: Guilford.
Mulgan examines a variety of recent technological innovations in telecommunications, including computers, fiber-optic cables, and satellites. He argues that these new developments should be seen not only as innovations in communication but also as being closely linked to new techniques of control. Some critical economic and political issues that will need to be addressed in the 1990s are also discussed.

(1984). *The 9 to 5 Survey on Women and Stress.* Cleveland: 9 to 5, National Association of Working Women.
This text presents the results of a comprehensive survey that focuses attention on the relatively unexplored hazards of psychosocial stress, its root causes, effects on health and well-being, and the methods of coping most effective for women.

Noble, David (1977). *American by Design: Science, Technology and the Rise of Corporate Capitalism.* New York: Alfred A. Knopf.
A discussion of the culture of engineering and its impact on the shape of our world. The author suggests that although the engineering community has successfully incorporated its own work into that of the capitalist enterprise, this affiliation is highly problematic.

Nye, David (1991). *Electrifying America: Social Meanings of a New Technology.* Cambridge, Mass.: Massachusetts Institute of Technology Press.
An analysis of the social and cultural impact of electricity on everyday life. Nye suggests that electricity's importance to Americans extends beyond the functional, and that society has used it to selectively redefine and restructure American culture.

O'Brien, Anne P. and Monique Ramionl (1989). "Given the Limitations of Technology Agreements for Women Workers, How Can Women Better Defend Their Interests in the Face of Technological Change?" In Kea Tijdens et al. (Eds.), *Women, Work and Computerization: Forming New Alliances* (pp. 181-188). North Holland: Elsevier Science Publishers.
The limits of technology agreements for female workers in trade union policies is discussed. Because most trade unions do not take into account the sexual division of labor, this paper maintains that it is up to women laborers to seek structural improvement in their unions by, among other routes, creating channels of information exchange among women.

Ogrim, Leikny (1989). "Decentralized System Development: Advantageous For Women?" In Kea Tijdens et al. (Eds.), *Women, Work and Computerization: Forming New Alliances* (pp. 171-180). North Holland: Elsevier Science Publishers.
This paper aims to contribute to a growing discussion on how decentralized system development can lead to increased influence for women over their own employment conditions.

Olerup, Agneta et al. (Eds.) (1985). *Women, Work, and Computerization: Opportunities and Disadvantages.* North Holland: Elsevier Science Publishers.
This collection of papers addresses the impact of computers on women and women's work. Topics covered include a description of the conference; the effect of computers

and new technology on office work; remote work; women and computers in industrial work; participation of women in system design; education of female computer professionals and engineers; and reports on women and computerization in western European countries.

Ormos, Marta and Maya Blameble (1989). "Strategies of Introduction of Office Automation in Mixed and Traditionally Female Jobs Within Two Work Units of the French Electricity and Gas Public Utility Companies." In Kea Tijdens et al. (Eds.), ***Women, Work and Computerization: Forming New Alliances*** **(pp. 49-56). North Holland: Elsevier.**
This paper examines the strategies of introduction of office automatization in two organizational settings.

Orvell, Miles (1982). "The Screen Revolution." ***Technology Review,*** **February/March, 40-47.**
Orvell insists that in order to understand the social, political, and personal effects of communications technologies, we must turn to the theories of Marshall McLuhan, which are described by the author.

Pacey, Arnold (1983). ***The Culture of Technology.*** **Cambridge, Mass.: Massachusetts Institute of Technology Press.**
The author poses the question of the neutrality of technology, and refutes it by suggesting that technology can only be understood within the social and economic context in which it is used. Interesting and persuasive case studies drawing upon various global uses of technology make this point quite well.

Palmer, Carolyn J. (1987). ***Effects of a Microcomputer-Intensive Residence Hall Environment on the Computer-Related Attitudes and Skills Of Undergraduate Students: A Study of Gender Differences.*** **Doctoral dissertation, University of Illinois at Urbana-Champaign.**
This dissertation examines the effects of a microcomputer-intensive environment on the computer-related attitudes and skills of students in residence halls and explores the extent to which these effects differ between men and women. The study suggests that access to computers and computer education in the residence hall environment may narrow the gender gap with respect to computers.

Penley, Constance and Andrew Ross (Eds.) (1991). ***Technoculture.*** **Minneapolis: University of Minnesota Press.**
This volume is presented in the knowledge that the odds are firmly stacked against the efforts of those committed to creating technological countercultures. Wary, on the one hand, of discussions that posit technology as a satanic mill of domination, and weary, on the other, of postmodern celebrations of the technological sublime, the editors aim at compiling a collection that moves toward a realistic assessment of the politics of advanced technologies.

Perkins, David (1985). "The Fingertip Effect: How Information Processing Shapes Thinking." ***Educational Researcher*****, August/September, 11-17.**
Perkins examines contemporary beliefs about the effect of information-processing technology (IPT) on thinking, finally concluding that current uses of IPT do not meet certain conditions for significantly reshaping thought, but that conditions may change as diversification spreads. (Note that this article was written before the emergence of hypermedia.)

Perritt, Henry Jr. (1989). "Government Information Goes On-line." ***Technology Review*****, December, 60-67.**
The author examines several current public-policy controversies surrounding information technologies.

Perry, Ruth and Lisa Greber (1990). "Women and Computers: An Introduction." ***Signs*****, 16(1), 74-101.**
If technological change is not simply inevitable, but in part determined by social, political, and economic forces, feminists must decipher how and to what extent technologies reflect or reinforce the patriarchal order. This article, first in a series to consider these issues in *Signs,* addresses the theoretical implications of technology in women's lives.

Radical Science Collective (1983). ***Autonomie: Infotech as Class Decomposition.*** **London: Free Association Books.**
This collection contains analyses of new technologies in the context of workers' experiences. Computer science and its applications in production is viewed as a new stage of the Taylorization of work. Articles deal with workers' attitudes to machinery in different historical phases and movements, and information technology is discussed in terms of a new stage in the class struggle.

Radical Science Collective (1985). ***Making Waves: The Politics of Communications.*** **London: Free Association Books.**
The essays in this collection explore the implications of communication technologies in the following areas: home work and computers, information technology and the "Third World", high-technology alternativism, and information technology and class. This collection is a gem for the critical scholar and an inspiration for the activist.

Rakow, Lana (1988). "Gendered Technology, Gendered Practice." ***Critical Studies in Mass Communication,*** **5(1), 57-70.**
Rakow critiques contemporary critical discussions of technology that ignore gender. She sees technology as gendered, and argues that technology is an area in which social practices are embedded and express and extend the construction of two asymmetric genders. She redefines discussions about technology to include gender and to suggest the implications for understanding gender and communication, focusing on two main bodies of theoretical work. The first includes theoretical arguments about technology, and the second includes the writing and research of feminists. She concludes with suggestions for our improved understanding of the relationships between gender, technology, and communication.

Rhodes, Frank (1990). "A System to Set Science Priorities." *Technology Review*, November, 21-23.
The federal government spends $62 billion a year in funding for science and technology, yet there is no coherent governmental system in place to review proposals or to justify how funds are allocated.

Richman, Dan (1990). "Image Processing the Hottest Advance in Archiving." *[Chicago] Tribune*, Section 19, 10.
Discussion of the recent changes in data storage technology, focussing on image processing. Image processing is the transformation of documents – letters, contracts, receipts, or checks – into an electronic form that allows compact, paperless storage and simultaneous access to many viewers.

Robins, Kevin and Frank Webster (1989). *The Technical Fix: Education, Computers and Industry*. New York: St. Martin's Press.
The authors make the point that technological innovation and the rationality of which it is expressive is deeply imbued with power relations; that is, technology is always shaped by prevailing values and power relations. The authors focus their discussion of technology on the context of innovations in education and suggest that the recent insistence on high-tech literacy extends and intensifies the processes of technocratic control.

Rogers, Everett M. (1986). *Communication Technology: The New Media in Society*. New York: The Free Press.
Rogers suggests that recent innovations in interactive technologies are causing a revolution in communication research because they demand a reconceptualization of the linear model of communication. This study traces the implications of interactive communication technologies on current research methodologies.

Ronell, Avital (1989). *The Telephone Book: Technology, Schizophrenia and Electric Speech*. Lincoln: University of Nebraska Press.
The phenomenology enthusiast's guide to the telephone and electric speech. Drawing upon the work of Heigedder, Ronell explores the many facets of the telephone asking such questions as "when does the telephone become what it is?" and "what does it mean to answer the telephone, to make oneself answerable to it in a situation whose gestural syntax already means yes...."

Rosenberg, Karen (1989). "In the Eye of the Beholder: Poetic Documentaries About Technology." *Technology Review*, February/March, 62-68.
The author, a critic of politics and culture, examines the poetic conceptualizations of technology of two Berlin filmmakers, Harmut Bitomsky and Harun Farocki. According to Rosenberg, their work assumes that culture has assimilated cliches about technology, and it tries to expose them using irony in narration, strange visual images, and startling juxtapositions.

Rosenberg, Ronni (1991). "Debunking Computer Literacy." ***Technology Review*****, January, 58-65.**
This article questions the enthusiasm for "computer literacy" programs currently in vogue in U.S. schools. The author maintains that these programs are, for the most part, counterproductive because they do not amount to meaningful job training, nor do they produce students who are informed about the role of computers in society.

Ross, Andrew (1991). ***Strange Weather: Culture, Science and Technology in the Age of Limits.*** **New York: Verso.**
Ross takes a cultural studies approach to the examination of the history of technocracy, focusing on topics such as scientists' position as gatekeepers and the latent power of lay skepticism about scientific and technological innovations. Ultimately, Ross argues for intervention on the part of cultural scholars in the debates influencing the shape of future technological changes.

Rothschild, Joan (Ed.) (1982). ***Women, Technology and Innovation.*** **New York: Pergamon.**
A collection of essays on diverse topics ranging from the relation of women to technology in ancient societies to women and modern electronics. A separate group of essays focuses on pedagogical issues relating to women and technology.

Rothschild, Joan (Ed.) (1983). ***Machina Ex Dea: Feminist Perspectives on Technology.*** **New York: Pergamon Press.**
Given that in our male-dominated culture, women tend to be the users of machines and technology and men their inventors, this collection of essays explores the historical, social, and psychological reasons for this anomaly. The writers suggest that women will become more involved in technology only to the extent that women become genuinely equal partners in the economy and the body politic.

Rothschild, Joan (1988). ***Teaching Technology from a Feminist Perspective: A Practical Guide.*** **New York: Pergamon Press.**
The author analyzes and synthesizes curriculum experiences that apply the new research on gender and technology to teaching about technology from feminist, historical, social, and philosophical perspectives. The book gives examples from actual courses that illustrate trends, issues, and ideas of teaching in the new field of women and technology. Twenty-two course syllabi are included in the appendix.

Samarajiva, R. and R. Mukherjee (1991). "Rules of the Road for the 'Electronic Highway': Glimmerings from the Dial-a-Porn Debate." (Paper presented to the 41st Annual Conference of the International Communication Association, Chicago, IL, May.)
This paper examines federal, state, regulatory, and telecommunication carrier actions shaping the institutional structure for the provision of audiotex services.

Schiebinger, Linda (1989). ***The Mind Has No Sex? Women in the Origins of Modern Science.*** **Cambridge, Mass.: Harvard University Press.**
The author of this fine volume writes with the aim to explore and refute the long-established tension between science and what Western culture has defined as "femininity." To address the tension, she analyzes the rise of modern science in Europe in

the 17th and 18th centuries, paying special attention to the circumstances that led to the exclusion of women.

Schmitt, Marilyn (1990). "Scholars Must Take the Lead in Computerization in the Humanities." ***The Chronicle of Higher Education*****, November, 21.**
Discussion of important issues posed by the electronic collection of information for scholars working in the humanities. Issues addressed include the problems in the distribution and retrieval of information in computerized data banks.

Schumacher, Ernest F. (1973). ***Small Is Beautiful: Economics As If People Mattered.*** **New York: Harper and Row.**
Schumacher makes the case for appropriate technology, arguing that bigger is not always better.

Schweickart, D. (1986). "What If.... Science and Technology in Feminist Utopias." ***Women's World*****, December, 54-56.**
This article offers four fascinating and useful readings of the ways in which science and technology are represented in four feminist utopian novels: *The Kin of Ata Are Waiting for You,* by Dorothy Bryant; *The Wanderground,* by Sally Gearhart; *Woman on the Edge of Time,* by Marge Piercy, and *The Dispossessed,* by Ursula Le Guin. The author maintains that these works offer insights into women's current ambivalence toward science and technology, and that women must recover their powers and faculties, which have atrophied as a result of the beginning of scientific reason.

Seigel, Lenny (1988). "Hong Kong: A Regional Case of Chip Production." ***Global Electronics*****, 89, 2.**
In Hong Kong, the first off-shore assembly site for the U.S. semiconductor industry and now a regional core of semiconductor chip production, multinational companies like Motorola employ only women workers to load chips into test equipment.

Selfe, Cynthia L. (1988). "The Humanization of Computers: Forget Technology, Remember Literacy." ***English Journal*****, October, 69-71.**
Discussion of the integration of computers into the English curriculum. Selfe cautions that as we rush to embrace computers and establish computer-supported writing labs, we must not let what we know about teaching literacy be eclipsed by what we need to teach about the new technology. An interesting discussion of the ways in which the demands of multilayered literacy complicates teaching.

Selfe, Cynthia L. and Paul Meyer (1991). "Testing Claims for On-line Conferences." ***Written Communication*****, 8(2), 163-192.**
In an exploratory study of gender and power relationships on one on-line conference, the authors found power differentials based on gender and high-profile status.

Siefert, Marsha, George Gerbner, and Janice Fischer (Eds.) (1989). ***The Information Gap: How Computers and Other New Communication Technologies Affect Social Distribution of Power.*** **New York: Oxford University Press.**
The articles in this book address the role of communication technology in enlarging availability as well as its tendency to exacerbate existing social inequities. These articles are geared toward documenting different types of technological patterns and barriers and their consequences for various social groups. The book contains several useful articles about gender and technology.

Slack, Jennifer Darryl (1984). ***Communication Technologies and Society: Conceptions of Causality and the Politics of Technological Intervention.*** **Norwood, N.J.: Ablex.**
Slack focuses on articulating a theoretical and practical model for understanding the ways in which social structures and practices are related to the development and use of communication technologies.

Slack, Jennifer Darryl, with Fred Fejes (1987). ***The Ideology of the Information Age.*** **Norwood, N.J.: Ablex.**
Slack argues that the information age is a contested terrain: what it is, how it is lived, how it is experienced, and how it is described vary greatly. Each of the contributors in this collection share the conviction that the terrain of the information age has developed and continues to develop in political, economic, and ideological struggle. The information age is an ongoing articulation of political, economic, and ideological arrangements and relations.

Slack, Jennifer Darryl (1989). "Contextualizing Technology: Communication Technologies and the Problem of Context." In Brenda Dervin, Lawrence Grossberg, Barbara J. O'Keefe, and Ellen Wartella (Eds.), ***Rethinking Communication, Volume 2: Paradigm Exemplars*** **(pp. 329-345). Newbury Park, Calif.: Sage.**
Slack uses a cultural studies approach to contextualizing communication technologies, appropriating Stuart Hall's conceptualization of articulation theory to examine the relational role of power in technology.

Sloat, B. (1990). "Perspectives on Women and the Sciences." ***Association for Women in Science Newsletter*****, 19(6), 4-5.**
Sloat, a professor of biology and founding director of the University of Michigan's Women in Science Program, offers her practical prescriptions for opening up the sciences to women at the university level.

Smart, Barry (1991). ***Modern Conditions, Postmodern Controversies.*** **New York: Routledge.**
In this book, Smart discusses some of the transformations in everyday life stemming from innovations in information technologies and changes in the modes of production. He stresses the need for alternative conceptualizations of the social organization of postindustrial society, and presents some interesting options.

Smith, M. R. (1991). "Not Invented Here – A Review of Technology in World Civilization: A Thousand-Year History, by Arnold Pacey." ***Technology Review*****, April, 76-77.**
This review discusses Pacey's historical perspective that the West's technological debt to other cultures is at least as great as the other way around. Pacey emphasizes that the most innovative societies are those that are responsive to new technical knowledge and "interrogate it on the basis of their own experience and knowledge of local conditions," which results in a technology dialogue. Smith maintains that this dialogic concept is an important insight for understanding the cultures of technology.

Sproull, Lee and Sara Kiesler (1991). ***Connections: New Ways of Working in the Networked Organization.*** **Cambridge, Mass.: Massachusetts Institute of Technology Press.**
An especially lucid discussion of the ways in which electronic communication media are being used in an organizational context. The authors demonstrate how computer-based communication can ease barriers and distortions in organizations and provide the possibilities for new alliances among people. A two-level framework for thinking about information technology is employed that is particularly useful for exploring the unanticipated consequences of information systems as they are actually used in social settings.

Stanley, Autumn (1983). "From Africa to America: Black Women Inventors." In Jan Zimmerman (Ed.), ***The Technological Woman: Interfacing with Tomorrow*** **(pp. 55-64). New York: Praeger.**
An interesting discussion of little-known African-American women inventors.

Stone, A. and J. S. Sanders (1986). ***The Neuter Computer: Computers for Girls and Boys.*** **New York: Neal-Schuman.**
This volume provides an overview of the computer gender gap, including fifty-six computer activities for children, ninety-six strategies for increasing girls' computer use, guidelines for planning and evaluating a computer equity program in a school, forms and questionnaires, and other resources. The introduction contains a Computer Neutrality Self-Test and describes the evidence, consequences, and causes of the computer gender gap. There is also a discussion of the relationship of math avoidance and software to computer equity.

Tarrant, Louise (1987). "Women and Information Poverty." ***Refractory Girl*****, October, 41-42.**
This essay addresses information technologies from an Australian context, maintaining that women in Australia live and work in an information-poor state. She asserts that questions of affirmative action and social equity must address the importance of the dynamic difference between having or not having information, and the relative social, economic, and political power or well-being of women.

Tijdens, Kea et al. (Eds.) (1989). *Women, Work and Computerization: Forming New Alliances.* New York: Elsevier Science Publishing.
This volume includes the papers and speeches of the third "Women, Work and Computerization" conference, organized by the International Federation of Information Processing. The conference was held in The Netherlands on April 27-29, 1988. The book is divided into five sections, following the themes of the workshops. The areas covered include organizational change, system design, training, empowering strategies, and the "Third World."

Traber, Michael (Ed.) (1986). *The Myth of the Information Revolution: Social and Ethical Implications of Communication Technology.* Beverly Hills: Sage.
The contributors of this volume argue that the so-called information revolution has occurred only for the few – i.e., those connected to transnational corporations and the military-industrial complex. The rest of us are still waiting for our lives to be significantly improved by new information technologies, and for most people in "Third World" countries, the information revolution has not even started.The authors argue that a way forward involves building a real information revolution through grass-roots networks rather than trying to seek access to corporate- or government-controlled media. Worth noting is Moema Viezzer's discussion of the women's movement for alternative communication in Latin America, and James D. Halloran's useful critique of mainstream communication research approaches to the study of new information technologies. With roots in the World Association for Christian Communication, the authors are sometimes too heavy-handed in their prescriptions of what constitute the most desirable moral and ethical responses to complex issues posed by new information technologies.

Tremblay, Diane (1989). "Technological Change, Internal Labour Markets and Women's Jobs: An Analysis Based on the Case of the Banking Sector." In Kea Tijdens et al. (Eds.), *Women, Work and Computerization: Forming New Alliances* (pp. 263-273). North Holland: Elsevier Science Publishing.
This paper is informed by theoretical positions denying technological determinism and maintaining that individual companies' human resource management plays an active role in modeling the outcome of computerization and technological change, especially with respect to women's employment conditions.

Trescott, Martha Moore (Ed.) (1979). *Dynamos and Virgins Revisited: Women and Technological Change in History.* Metuchen, New Jersey: Scarecrow Press.
This volume is divided into two parts. Part I looks at women as active agents in technological change, such as women inventors, engineers, scientists, and entrepreneurs. Part II focuses on the impact of technological change on women in the domestic sphere. Interesting essay on gender-stereotyped toys in the U.S. from 1920 to 1940.

Tsipis, Kosta (1990). "Time for Rebirth of Civilian Research and Development." *Technology Review*, November, 11-13.
Tsipis makes the case for increased civilian involvement in research and development, arguing that this will contribute positively to solving U.S. economic problems.

Tuana, Nancy (Ed.) (1989). *Feminism and Science*. Bloomington: Indiana University Press.
This book, a compilation of two special issues of *Hypatia: A Journal of Feminist Philosophy,* offers a multitude of feminist intellectual perspectives on science. These critiques focus on the ideologies, politics, epistemologies, economies, and metaphysics of traditional science.

Turkle, Sherry (1980). "Computer as Rorschach." *Society*, 17-24.
Turkle explores the social roles that the computer plays, not as a direct result of what they do, but because of the relationships people form with computers. She looks at the computer as a metaphor and as a projective medium, suggesting that this subjective side of the computer is relevant to understanding issues concerning computing and public life.

Turkle, Sherry (1984). *The Second Self: Computers and the Human Spirit*. New York: Simon and Schuster.
A study of the impact of computers, focusing on the role computers play in child development, on how adults interact with one another, and on the way we think about ourselves. Turkle's research is based on extensive fieldwork with children, students, "hackers," programmers, and artificial intelligence researchers.

Turkle, Sherry (1984). "Women and Computer Programming: A Different Approach." *Technology Review*, November/December, 48-52.
An earlier and less sophisticated version of her later essay for *Signs* on computer programming and epistemological pluralism, this essay covers the same ground, calling for a more inclusive computing environment.

Turkle, Sherry and Seymour Papert (1990). "Epistemological Pluralism: Styles and Voices Within the Computer Culture." *Signs*, 16(1), 128-157.
This article explores two approaches to computer programming – formal and concrete – and uses Gilligan's work to analyze their gendered natures. The authors suggest that the concrete approach, more favored by females, reflects a preferred approach to knowledge and that epistemological pluralism is a necessary condition for a more inclusive computer culture.

Urquidi, V. L. (Ed.) (1979). *Science and Technology in Development Planning: Science, Technology and Global Problems*. New York: Pergamon Press.
In this somewhat dated collection of papers from various United Nations-sponsored events, the all-male, Western contributors explore the changing roles of science and technology in global planning and "development."

United States Commission on Civil Rights (1983). *Women and Minorities in High Technology*. (Testimony from hearing held in San Jose, Calif., September 20-21, 1982.) Washington, D.C.: U.S. Government Printing Office.
The purpose of these hearings was to examine the high-technology industry and the opportunities for business development and employment for women and minorities. Other concerns were evaluation of existing and proposed strategies for their increased involvement and focus on the roles of federal, state, and local governments in this endeavor.

Vare, Ethlie and G. Ptacek (1987). *Mothers of Invention From the Bra to the Bomb: Forgotten Women and Their Unforgettable Ideas.* New York: William Morrow.
This collection of brief herstories of women and their inventions is a necessary corrective to malestream accounts of the "progress of men" by proving that being female does not prevent one from pursuing technological activities. The inventors documented include Ada Lovelace, who engineered the prototype computer, Grace Murray Hopper, who developed the earliest computer software, and other scientists, healers, housewives, nuns, secretaries, and actresses.

Slesin, L. (1991). "PMFs and Pregnancy: Clues Emerge, Conflicts Persist," *VDT News.*
Discussion of the effects of pulsed magnetic fields (PMFs) on pregnancy. The newsletter, VDT News, serves as a forum for the coverage of VDT (video display terminal) health and safety issues, including research on reproductive risks, and other health effects of VDT-type radiation, outbreaks of and treatment for repetition strain injuries, vision problems, regulatory and legislative actions, and office ergonomics.

Verhoef, J. (1989). "Realizing Training Programmes for Women on Informatics." In Kea Tijdens et al. (Eds.), *Women, Work and Computerization: Forming New Alliances* (pp. 211-216). North Holland: Elsevier Science Publishers.
This paper presents the results of a vocational training program designed for women who want to return to the labor market after having children. The paper focuses on the following areas: the practical demands of educational programs for women, the specific terms of training contents, and personal computer use.

Volst, Angelika and Ina Wagner (1989). "Polarized Patterns: Effects of Computerization on Women's Career Opportunities. "In Kea Tijdens et al. (Eds.), *Women, Work and Computerization: Forming New Alliances* (pp. 67-76). North Holland: Elsevier Science Publishers.
This paper combines an analysis of the role of computers in reinforcing the flexibility of work organizations with a discussion of changes in women's participative behavior in the labor market, concluding that both employers' strategies and women's patterns of access to the labor market result in an increasing polarization of career opportunities for women.

Wajcman, Judy (1991). *Feminism Confronts Technology.* University Park: The Pennsylvania State University Press.
Wajcman writes about the gendered character of technology, focusing on such areas as the impact of production technologies, domestic technologies, and the built environment. The first chapter lays out a clear discussion of feminist theories of science and technology.

Webster, Fred and Kevin Robins (1986). *Information Technology: A Luddite Analysis.* Norwood, N.J.: Ablex Publishing Corporation.
Although the popular conception of Luddism portrays it as unintelligent, often violent, indiscriminate, backward-looking, opposed to progress, and futile, the authors of this volume argue otherwise. Although Luddism has been dismissed as a primitive form of resistance, appropriate to "societies where the patterns of industrialization were incomplete," the authors put forward a positive interpretation of Luddism as "an

alternative political economy and morality to that of *laissez-faire* because it carries an ethical response in opposition to the changes wrought upon society by the dispassionate logic of industrial capitalism." The book reveals the social relations that information technology embodies, and the forces that account for its genesis, adoption, and use.

Weil, V. et al. (Eds.) (1989). *Owning Scientific and Technical Information: Value and Ethical Issues.* New Brunswick: Rutgers University Press.
The papers in this volume investigate the foundations of the intellectual property system. Theoretical questions raised from the perspectives of law, philosophy, and economics are explored, along with an examination of the actual functioning of the intellectual property system. Ethical issues such as fairness in the allocation of benefits and public access to new technology and knowledge are addressed.

Weinberg, S. (1984). *Computer Phobia.* Wayne, Penn.: Banbury Books, Inc.
This volume, which is based on interviews with over 1,200 so-called computerphobics, provides clues for easing the transition to computer use. Designed as a guide to give clear, nonthreatening examples of coping with an increasingly wired society, this book unfortunately oversimplifies the complex and contradictory social rules that contribute to unequal access and enthusiasm for electronic media.

Weinberg, S. (1987). "Expanding Access to Technology: Computer Equity for Women." In B. D. Wright et al. (Eds.), *Women, Work and Technology: Transformations* (pp. 281-290). Ann Arbor: University of Michigan Press.
This article presents some practical approaches toward fostering a more inclusive computer community.

Weizenbaum, Joseph (1976). *Computer Power and Human Reason: From Judgement to Calculation.* San Francisco: W. H. Freeman and Co.
The author makes two main arguments in this book: first, that there are important differences between people and machines, and second, that there are certain tasks computers should not be allowed to do, regardless of whether computers can be made to do them.

Werneke, Diane (1984). *Microelectronics and Office Jobs: Impact of the Chip on Women's Employment.* London: International Labor Office.
This work centers on the effect of microelectronic technology on women in the office environment. New office technology is described and its effect on work content and organization is assessed. Emphasis is on the U.S., but information on other countries is presented also.

Westlander, Gunnela and Bjorn Magnusson (1988). "Swedish Women and New Technology." ***Women and Health*****, 13(3-4), 95-116**
This article focuses on the overall situation of women in Sweden with respect to computer-based technology. The information and analysis provided is based on a survey of computer use in Sweden carried out in June 1984 by Statistics Sweden. The researchers found that although women are involved in new technology in Sweden to a great extent, there is male dominance in both the initiation and development of new technology. Part of the reason for male dominance may be not only the nature of new technology itself but also the social roles that females and males stereotypically assume in the workplace.

Whicker, Marcia Lynn and Jennie Jacobs Kronenfeld (1986). ***Sex Role Changes: Technology, Politics and Policy*****. New York: Praeger.**
The authors explicate their four-stage technology-based theory of social change. They suggest that technology defines the physically feasible, which in turn defines social organization and personal interaction. The four stages are as follows: First, technological innovations are developed and distributed. Second, social norms and values change in adaptation to the expanded opportunities made possible by the technological innovation. Third, pressure from changing behavior and norms builds in the political system, creating political movements and interest group demands. Fourth, legal and policy changes may result. This general theory of technology-driven social change is applied to the changing roles of women and changing male-female relationships. Two major factors relating to social change are birth control and production technologies.

Whole Earth Review (1991). ***Questioning Technology*****, 73.**
An entire issue addressing the proliferation of new information technologies, with special attention paid to the social and cultural aspects of their use. Writers published in this issue include Linda Garcia, Patricia Schuman, Langdon Winner, and Jerry Mander.

Williams, Fredrick (Ed.) (1988). ***Measuring the Information Society*****. Newbury Park, Calif.: Sage.**
This collection of research reports attempts to analyze facets of the so-called information society, using Texas as a case in point. Topics addressed include the information society as an object of study, the "technopolis" concept, science and technology policy, public attitudes toward science and technology, and education in the information age.

Winner, Langdon (1986). ***The Whale and the Reactor: A Search for Limits in an Age of High Technology*****. Chicago: University of Chicago Press.**
Winner explores the meanings of technology for the way we live. By moving beyond the obvious facts of instrumentality to the study of the politics of technical objects, the author develops a political philosophy of technology. There are useful discussions of appropriate technology and the politics of language as well as a critique of the so-called computer revolution.

Winograd, Terry and Fernando Flores (1985). ***Understanding Computers and Cognition: A New Foundation for Design*****. Norwood, N.J.: Ablex.**
Winograd and Flores conduct a detailed critique of the rationalist paradigm for understanding embodied perceptual and language systems and for designing computers that can function as prostheses in human projects. Drawing on Heidegger, Gadamer,

Maturána, and others, Winograd and Flores develop a doctrine of interdependence of interpreter and interpreted, which are not discrete and independent entities. "Structure-determined systems" with histories shaped through processes of "structural coupling" give a better approach to perception than doctrines of representation.

Winston, Brian (1986). *Misunderstanding Media.* Cambridge, Mass.: Harvard University Press.
This book challenges the dominant rhetoric celebrating the so-called information "revolution" and attempts to historically situate media technologies. Winston's approach involves examining the ways technologies are invented and diffused, with particular emphasis on television.

Women in Publishing (Eds.) (1987). *Reviewing the Reviews.* London: The Journeyman Press.
Stemming from a meeting of "Women in Publishing" in June 1985 at which the issue of women's books and book reviews arose, this slim volume brilliantly and systematically addresses the question of women's place on the book review pages. The researchers include comments and opinions from individuals working in the publishing industry such as publishers, literary editors, booksellers, librarians, and authors that reveal attitudes towards the publication of women's writing. Among other alarming results, the researchers discover the fact that the most influential publications show the most bias against women.

(1988). *Women and Minorities in Science and Engineering.* Washington, D.C., National Science Foundation.
A lucid discussion of where women and minorities are in science and engineering. For example, in 1986, 28% of the computer specialists in the United States were women, compared with 13% of the practitioners in the physical sciences, 22% in the life sciences, and 3% of the practicing engineers. Four percent of all the women employed in computer science were Black; 5.4% were Asian. Salaries for women were lower than those of men across all fields of science and engineering, although the differential was less in computer science than in other fields. In the sciences, salaries for women averaged 76% of the salaries for men across the board; among engineers, women's salaries were 84% of men's; among computer specialists, "the fastest-growing field for both men and women during the eighties," women's salaries averaged 86% of men's.

(1985). "Women, Work and Computerization: Opportunities and Disadvantages," In A. Olerup, L. Schneider, and E. Monod (Eds.). *The First Working Conference on Women, Work and Computerization*, Riva del Sol, Tuscany, Italy. New York: Elsevier Science Publishers.
These papers address the effect of computers on women and women's work. The first of seven parts describes the conference, its background, objectives, and results. The remaining sections consider the effect of computers and new technology on office work; remote work or telecomputing; women and computers in industrial work; participation of women in systems design; education of female computer professionals and engineers; and reports on women and computerization in Western European countries.

Wright, Barbara Drygulski et al. (Eds.) (1987). *Women, Work and Technology: Transformations*. Ann Arbor: The University of Michigan Press.
The subject of this book is technological development and its relationship to women workers. Focusing on the United States and Western Europe, the authors recognize that throughout the world, women labor in many settings for many different kinds of rewards, and a truly comprehensive definition of women's work must include reproduction and agricultural and household labor, as well as paid employment outside the home.

Wright, Barbara Drygulski (1987). "Women, Work and the University-Affiliated Technology Park." In Barbara Drygulski Wright et al. (Eds.), *Women, Work and Technology: Transformations* (pp. 352-370). Ann Arbor: University of Michigan Press.
At a time when feminism, affirmative action, and women's studies have made the university more open to women, science and technology remain one of the last male preserves. Starting from this premise, the author considers the male-dominated area of corporate-sponsored university "technology parks," detailing the effect on women of being left out of their planning and development.

Yates, Joanne A. (Ed.) (1989). *Control Through Communication: The Rise of Systems in American Management*. Baltimore: Johns Hopkins University Press.
Yates documented and analyzed the introduction of, adoption of, and responses to new communication technologies in organizational settings. Her technique of comparative case studies is insightful. By examining in detail the history of three individual businesses –The Illinois Central Railroad, Scovill Manufacturing Company, and E. I. Du Pont de Nemours and Company – she is able to understand the human and organizational contexts in which change came to the modern economy. By simultaneously analyzing the coming of the new office technologies and the rise of systematic management, she is able to place her case studies in the larger setting of the capitalist system as a whole.

Yourdon, Edward (1986). *Nations at Risk: The Impact of the Computer Revolution*. New York: Yourdon Press.
This alarmist, extremely reactionary book addresses precisely how the computer revolution puts "our nation at greater and greater [economic] risk each day."

Zimmerman, Jan (Ed.) (1983). *The Technological Woman: Interfacing with Tomorrow*. New York: Praeger.
This pioneering work provides a feminist critique of technology. Zimmerman, in a comprehensive set of essays, covers a wide range of issues from household technologies to abortion and reproductive technologies, in addition to dealing with office automation, jobs in high technology organizations, and computer education for girls.

Zimmerman, Jan (1983). "A Feminist Perspective on Technology and the Future." In Joan Rothschild (Ed.), *Machina Ex Dea: Feminist Perspectives on Technology*. New York: Pergamon Press.
Zimmerman articulates a feminist position on technology, arguing that women must seek to take control of new technologies for ourselves.

Zimmerman, Jan (1986). *Once Upon the Future: A Woman's Guide to Tomorrow's Technology*. London: Routledge and Kegan Paul.
This volume explores the world of technology from a feminist's and a woman's point of view. The author discusses the ways and reasons women suffer under the invisible tyranny of technological things as well as why taking control of technology is so crucial for women trying to take control of their own lives.

Zuboff, Shoshana (1984). *In the Age of the Smart Machine: The Future of Work and Power*. New York: Basic Books.
Computer-based technologies are not neutral; they embody essential characteristics that are bound to alter the nature of work in our factories and offices and among workers, professionals, and managers. This book is an effort to understand the deep structure of the choices provided by these technologies, and the historical, psychological, and organizational forces that imbue our conduct and sensibility.

Except as noted, all addresses are at the University of Illinois at Urbana-Champaign

Joan Alster,
Research Programmer,
Computing Services Office

Carole Appel,
Senior Editor,
University of Illinois Press

Marie Banich,
Associate Professor,
Psychology,
Beckman Institute

Jenny Barrett,
Research Programmer,
Computer-Based Education Research Laboratory

Colleen Bushell,
Research Programmer,
National Center for Supercomputing Applications

Kathleen Chmelewski,
Assistant Professor,
Photography and Graphic Design, School of Art and Design

Kathleen Cloud,
Director, Women in International Development

Ramona Curry,
Assistant Professor,
English

Maureen Ebben,
Doctoral candidate,
Speech Communication

Laura Ege,
Higher Education Representative,
Apple Computers

Karolyn Eisenstein,
Deputy Director,
Science and Technology Center for Superconductivity

Leigh Estabrook,
Dean, School of Library and Information Science

Monica Fortner,
Senior Specialist in Automated Education Computer-Based Education Research Lab

Susan Greendorfer,
Professor, Kinesiology

Gail Hawisher,
Associate Professor,
English; Director, Center for Writing Studies

Yamuna Kachru,
Professor, Linguistics

Jo Kibbee,
Reference Library Head,
University Library

Nori I. Komorita,
Associate Professor and Director, College of Nursing

Cheris Kramarae,
LAS Jubilee Professor,
Speech Communication,
Sociology, Linguistics,
Women's Studies

Susan Lamb,
Associate Professor,
Physics and Astronomy

Melanie Loots,
Associate Director of Applications,
National Center for Supercomputing Applications

Radha Nandkumar,
Research Scientist,
National Center for Supercomputing Applications

Bea Nettles,
Professor, School of Art and Design; Program Chair, Photography

Jean Peterson,
Associate Professor, Human Development and Family Studies

Nora Sabelli,
Senior Research Scientist, National Center for Supercomputing Applications

Linda C. Smith,
Associate Professor, Library and Information Science

Beth Stafford-Vaughan,
Women's Studies/WID Librarian, University Library

H. Jeanie Taylor,
Associate Director, Center for Advanced Study

Phyllis Vanlandingham,
Assistant Director, Women's Studies Program

Ellen Wartella,
Professor, Institute of Communications Research

Sarah Wasserman,
Associate Director, Beckman Institute for Advanced Science and Technology

Liesel Wildhagen,
Staff Associate,Center for Advanced Study

Betsy Wilson,
Undergraduate Librarian University Library (currently Associate Director of Libraries for Public Service, University of Washington)

Marie T. Banich is an Associate Professor in the Department of Psychology with an appointment in the Beckman Institute for Advanced Science and Technology at the University of Illinois at Urbana-Champaign. Her research in cognitive neuroscience examines the way the two hemispheres of the brain communicate. Her involvement in WITS stems from an interest in how information is communicated in systems, whether composed from neurons or microchips, and from an appreciation that science as a cultural institution is value laden. (mbanich@s.psych.uiuc.edu)

Kathleen Chmelewski is Assistant Professor of Photography and Graphic Design in the School of Art and Design, University of Illinois at Urbana-Champaign. Her research focuses on digital imaging for visual communications, and on the ethical and ecological implications of new technologies used for representation. (kathleen @ux1.cso.uiuc.edu)

Maureen Ebben is a doctoral candidate in Speech Communication at the University of Illinois at Urbana-Champaign and research assistant for the WITS colloquium. Her dissertation addresses the question of whether the asymmetrical conversational practices for women and men in face-to-face communication reproduce themselves in the context of electronic communication. She serves as the coordinator of the Graduate Student Interest Group of WITS and is a member of the WITS advisory board. (ebben@vmd.cso.uiuc.edu)

Nan Goggin is Assistant Professor of Graphic Design, School of Art and Design, University of Illinois at Urbana-Champaign. (goggin@uxa.cso.uiuc.edu)

Phyllis Hall is Staff Director of Publishing Services, Institute of Electrical and Electronics Engineers (320,000 members, 5% women), and former Senior Vice President of Pergamon Press, a major publisher of academic journals. (p.hall@ieee.org)

Gail Hawisher is Associate Professor of English, and Director, Center for Writing Studies, University of Illinois at Urbana-Champaign. She is coeditor of the journal *Computers and Composition: A Journal for Teachers of Writing,* and of the book *Evolving Perspectives on Computers and Composition Studies: Questions for the 1990s*. (hawisher@uiuc.edu)

H. Patricia Hynes is Director of the Institute of Women and Technology and an adjunct professor of Environmental Policy in the Department of Urban Studies and Planning at the Massachusetts Institute of Technology. Her research focuses on women, technology, and the environment. Her books include *The Recurring Silent Spring*, a book about Rachel Carson, and policy on pesticides, genetic engineering in agriculture, and the new reproductive technologies.

Jo Kibbee is Head of Central Reference Services in the University Library, University of Illinois at Urbana-Champaign. In the spring of 1992 she received funding to conduct research on library applications of the U.K.'s Joint Academic Network (JANET). (jkibbee@vmd.cso.uiuc.edu)

Cheris Kramarae is Jubilee Professor of Liberal Arts and Sciences and Professor of Speech Communication, Sociology, Women's Studies, and Linguistics at the University of Illinois at Urbana-Champaign, and a cofounder of WITS. She is the author or coeditor of ten books on women, language and feminist scholarship, including *Technology and Women's Voices*. She and Dale Spender are coeditors of the *International Encyclopedia of Women's Studies*, in preparation. (cheris@uiuc.edu)

Maria Mastronardi is a doctoral candidate in Speech Communication, University of Illinois at Urbana-Champaign. Her research interest is in feminist cultural studies and particularly in the ways in which female sexuality gets articulated, practiced, and discursively constructed in popular cultural forms.

Ann Okerson is Director, Office of Scientific and Academic Publishing, Association of Research Libraries, Washington, D.C. In her position, Okerson is actively involved with the evolution of academic publishing in the electronic age. (okerson@umdc.umd.edu)

Sandy Osterbur is a secretary at the Center for Advanced Study, University of Illinois at Urbana-Champaign. During the year she was involved in keeping the WITS colloquium arrangements on schedule, and she was instrumental in the correcting and editing of this volume.

Dale Spender, scholar-at-large, Australia, is a cofounder of WITS and a graduate of the Universities of Sydney and London. She is a feminist whose major research interest (in more than twenty books) has been to document the absence of a fair hearing for women and to assess the implications of this for language, literature, history, technology, and the politics of knowledge in general. She was the founding editor of *Women's Studies International Forum* and of Pandora Press in England. She has taught in universities in many countries.

Judy Smith is Project Director of WORD (Women's Opportunity and Resource Development Inc.) in Missoula, Montana. WORD is involved in working on economic development and welfare reform for women.

H. Jeanie Taylor is Associate Director of the Center for Advanced Study, University of Illinois at Urbana-Champaign, and a cofounder of WITS. She is a member of the Women in International Development Executive Committee and the Women's Studies General Council, and a graduate student in speech communication. (jeanietc@ux1.cso.uiuc.edu)

Betsy Wilson, formerly Undergraduate Librarian, University of Illinois at Urbana-Champaign, is currently Associate Director of Libraries for Public Services at the University of Washington in Seattle, Washington. (betsyw@u.washington.edu)

Also contributing, the Members of WITS.